Spora Stories presents

PANDORA'S BOX
BY ADE SOLANKE

Supported using public funding by
**ARTS COUNCIL
ENGLAND**

LOTTERY FUNDED

Pandora's Box is supported by the Unity Theatre Trust

Spora Stories

SPORA STORIES

We create original drama for stage a d screen, telling the dynamic stories c the African diaspora. We're inspired b the vigour, ambition and global impact of both Nigerian popular cinema and of contemporary British theatre. Our passion is for great stories, well told.

Our stories deliver the most compelling characters in the most gripping situations. Africans, Europeans, 'Afropeans' ... British-Africans, African-Americans, 'Afro-politans' ... Londoners in Lagos, Lagosians in London ... the teeming traffic of peoples and stories jostling for expression in the swirl of the 21st-century world. The sparks – and stories – flying from the collision between Africa and Europe: close encounters of the creative kind. 'One hand can't clap,' goes the African saying. What kind of stories leap out from this 'clap' between worlds?

Our vision is to harness in drama these exciting times: to tap into the wave of Afro-optimism bubbling across the continent and the diaspora; to develop new, entertaining and exciting contemporary work; and to reflect – and dissect – African experience in modern Britain, America and Africa.

'We carry within us the wonders we seek without us, There is all Africa and her prodigies in us.'
Sir Thomas Browne, *Religio Medici*, 1642

www.sporastories.com | info@sporastories.com
@sporastories

Spora Stories wishes to extend its grateful thanks to:

The Solankes, Diane Abbott MP, Richard Taylor OBE, Olu Alake, Professor Osita Okagbue, Dr. Sunday Popo-ola, Caroline Allotey-Annan, Sola Adeyemi, Lookman Sanusi, Jon Harris, Shade Oladiti, David Duchin, Rhian Kennedy, Thomas Kell, Jonathan Kennedy, Tayo Aluko, Sherry De Wynter, Lillian Nevins, David Faulkner, Waka Waka North East, Claire Symonds, Charles Small, Oluwatoyin Odunsi, Godfrey Brandt, Jenny Killick, Neil Darlison, Pete Staves and all at ACE, Unity Theatre Trust, Peggy Ramsay Foundation, AHRC, The British Council, Kim Morgan PR, Lydia Wharf, Sophia Jackson/Afridiziak Theatre News, Rachel Fox, Dan Bates, Tom Fleming, Bevis Gooden and Luton Black Men Community Group, all our partner venues and Oberon Books.

PANDORA'S BOX
BY ADE SOLANKE

CAST

ANYEBE ANTEYI	Tope
TUNDE EUBA	Baba
EDWARD KAGUTUZI	Timi
CHINWE NWOKOLO	Bev
YETUNDE ODUWOLE	Sis Ronke
TOMI OGUNJOBI	Mama Ronke
AMOUR OWOLABI	Principal Osun
ESTHER UWEJEYAH	Toyin

CREATIVE TEAM

ADE SOLANKE	Playwright/Producer
JON HARRIS	Co-Producer
SHADE OLADITI	Director
MADELEINE KLUDJE	Assistant Director
LOOKMAN SANUSI	Associate Producer
SUZANNE GORMAN	Participation Producer
DAVID DUCHIN	Production Manager
RHIAN KENNEDY	Stage Manager
SARA RHODES-CANNING	Assistant Stage Manager
MOJI BAMTEFA	Costumes
KIM MORGAN PR	Press, Marketing and audience development
LYDIA WHARF	Regional press and marketing
AFRIDIZIAK THEATRE NEWS	Social Media Consultants

CAST

TUNDE EUBA Baba
Tunde is an actor/director/writer/facilitator who has enjoyed a long and varied career in theatre. Starting out as an actor, he later explored other "areas of artistic expression" and turned his hand to writing, directing and more recently, photography. After a ten year break from touring, Tunde is 'back on the road again', fittingly retrieving his role of Baba six years after his appearance in the very first reading of *Pandora's Box* at the Almeida Theatre.

CHINWE NWOKOLO Bev
Chinwe is an actress from South London.
She studied entertainment journalism but after playing a role in a short film at university, she turned to acting. After graduating, she enrolled at a weekend drama school where she began her career. Credits include: *West 10 LDN* (BBC Three), *My Territory* (Soho Theatre), *The Gods Are Not To Blame* (Young Vic theatre) and most recently *House of Corrections* (Riverside Studios).

ANYEBE ANTEYI Tope
Anyebe Godwin Anteyi is an actor originally from South London. He has performed at many venues and has also enjoyed two successfully sold out tours with State of Play Arts. Anyebe trained at Rose Bruford College and is also a member of Theatre Royal Stratford East's Young Artists Lab most recently performing in their Summer 2014 studio season. His credits include: *G.I Joe in Dorset* (Tour & Mary Shelley Theatre), *Flat Lives* (Theatre Royal Stratford East), *Family 2.0* (The Cockpit Theatre) and *Misidentity* (Lost Theatre).

EDWARD KAGUTUZI Timi
Edward trained at Identity Drama school, Theatre Studies A-Level. Credits include: Theatre – *House of Corrections* (Bola Agbaje), *Covered* (Daniel Bailey). Television – *Law and Order UK* (ITV), *Brixton Hill Cop* (Triple Threat Media), *Mo Ali* (Dubplate Drama, Channel 4). Film – *The Mirror Boy* (OH TV), *Illegal Activity* (Kingdom Vision Pictures). Awards – Best Young Actor (African Movie Academy Awards), Best Actor (BEFFTA).

YETUNDE ODUWOLE Sis Ronke

Yetunde trained at Central School of Speech and Drama, Stella Alder New York, Goldsmiths College and City Lit. She has worked with Tiata Fahodzi, Talawa Theatre, Royal Court Theatre. Credits include: *Adulto Orgasmo* (Lion 7 Unicorn Theatre), *Torn* (Arcola Theatre), *The New Boss* (Broadway Theatre), *Hackney Streets* (Rosemary Branch Theatre), *The Harlot* (Coronet Theatre), *The Wedlock Of the Gods* (Cochrane Theatre), *Meet the Adebanjos* (Hackney Empire, Catford Broadway Theatre and the OHTV television series), *Pandora's Box* (Arcola Theatre), *Youngers* (E4) and various short films.

ESTHER UWEJEYAH Toyin

Esther is a member of Fragments Theatre Company. She played Pontius Pilate in their recent adaptation of *The Master and Margarita*. Recently she played Nina in *Satanic Panic* in a successful run at the Drayton Arms Theatre. A Modern Drama Graduate (Brunel), Esther's work can also be found on screen having appeared as Sabrina in the popular web series *Brothers with No Game* and as Anne in the web series *Redemptions End*.

AMOUR OWOLABI Principal Osun

Amour trained at The Actors Centre, The Actors Lab and Identity Drama School. Amour is a BEFTA and LA-WEB award winner. Recent television and film includes: *Dignity Of Difference* (BBC), *The MehmeFemi's*, *Hunting For Hubbies*; *Silent Witness* (BBC); *Fall Out* (Ch4); *Sprint*; *GT Assure*; *Nigerian Heritage*; *Bouquet*; *Shooting Stars* (BBC); *All About The Mckenzies*; *Daarsat*; *Rayban*; *Unspoken series 1 & 2*; *Sainsbury's*; *Displaced Diagetics*; *Shattered Hearts*; *MTV*. Amour has been presenting a live TV show on BEN TV for the past three years.

TOMI OGUNJOBI Mama Ronke

Tomi is a graduate of Theatre Arts, University of Ibadan, Nigeria, specialising in acting, singing, dance and movement. Tomi has worked with Ola Rotimi, Femi Osofisan, Dapo Adelugba, Bayo Oduneye, Bassey Effiong, Ben Tomoloju, Chuck Mike and Rufus Norris. Recent credits include: *Our Husband has Gone Mad Again* by Ola Rotimi, *Where the Devils Dwell* by Rhiannon Tise, Royal Court Young People's Theatre London and *Muje-muje* by Ben Tomoloju.

CREATIVE TEAM

ADE SOLANKE Playwright/Producer
Ade Solanke is an award-winning playwright and screenwriter. Her company, Spora Stories, makes original, contemporary drama telling the dynamic stories of the 'Afrospora,' or African diaspora.

Spora produced *Pandora's Box*, her acclaimed, sell-out debut play at London's Arcola Theatre, which was nominated for Best New Play in the 2012 Off West End Awards. It won Best Playwright at both the African Film Awards and Nigerian Entertainment Awards 2012 and was shortlisted for the $100,000 Nigeria Prize for Literature 2014, Africa's biggest literary award.

Her plays have been performed in leading festivals of new writing at the Almeida Theatre, the Young Vic and Rich Mix, and she's a member of Soho Theatre's Writers' Hub, and has run drama courses at Soho Theatre and the Royal Court.

Ade is a judge for the Nollywood Movies Awards (NMA) in Lagos and works with other festivals and theatre and film projects around the world. Her screenplays have been both quarter-finalists and semi-finalists in the US Academy's Nicholl Screenwriting contest. In LA, she was a story analyst for several Hollywood Studios, including Sundance, New Line and Disney.

She has developed and delivered scriptwriting courses and masterclasses at Goldsmiths College, University of London, London Screenwriters Workshop, BOB Expo in Abuja, Pan-Atlantic University, Lagos, Africa International Film Festival (AFRIFF), Calabar, and the African Womens' Film Forum in Accra, Ghana. She runs writing training courses internationally with the British Council. She was the British Film Institute's first Writer-in-Residence, with the support of the Royal Literary Fund, of which she is a fellow, and is a member of the BFI's African Odysseys Committee, which programmes African films at the UK's National Film Theatre. Earlier in her career, she was voted 'London's Top Youth Entrepreneur' for her writing business.

Ade has an MFA in Film and Television (Screenwriting) from the University of Southern California (USC) School of Cinematic Arts where she was a Fulbright Fellow and Phi Beta Kappa International Scholar. She has an Honours Degree in English Literature from the University of Sheffield, and a PG Diploma in Creative Writing from Goldsmiths, University of London, where she was recently AHRC-funded Writer-in-Residence at the Department of Theatre and Performance's Pinter Centre. She tweets @sporastories.

JON HARRIS Co-producer
Jon is a freelance arts management teacher, consultant, accountant and business psychologist. He started his career in the arts, producing theatre shows in the West End and on tour all over the world, and subsequently trained and coached communications skills and business skills in a wide variety of industries, especially professional services. He is Associate Tutor at Goldsmiths' University Institute for Creative and Cultural Entrepreneurship and principal tutor in Arts Management at City Lit.

SHADE OLADITI Director
Shade recent work includes directing one-woman show *In My Shoes* at the Millfield Theatre; sitcom *Meet the Adebanjos* (adapted for the stage) at Catford Broadway and Hackney Empire; various roles on season 2 of *Meet the Adebanjos*; directing Quincy's *Scrooge*, a loose adaptation of *Christmas Carol*. Shade also works as a facilitator for Face Front Inclusive Theatre on their 'Play in a Day' programme for Year 7 pupils.

MADELEINE KLUDJE Assistant Director
Madeleine trained at the Brit School of the Performing Arts and also has a Music and Arts Management and Marketing degree. She has assisted on numerous projects at the Young Vic including a full scale parallel production of *The Scottsboro Boys* with the Young Vic's under 18 participants. Madeleine has also assisted at Talawa Theatre Company, directing Theresa Ikoko's debut play *Normal* for Talawa Firsts. She'll be assisting Dawn Reid at Theatre Royal Stratford East in Autumn 2014.

LOOKMAN SANUSI Associate Producer
Lookman is an artist, journalist, writer, producer and director, working in both Nigeria and the UK. His production credits include: *Raisin in the Sun, A View from the Bridge, The Man Who Never Died, Kongi's Harvest, Trials of Brother Jero, The Gods are Not to Blame*. In 2012, he directed Ola Rotimi's *Our Husband has gone Mad Again* which toured in London. He is currently the Creative Director of Bubbles FM, a digital radio station in London dedicated to the Arts, Lifestyle and Entertainment.

SUZANNE GORMAN Participation Producer
Suzanne is a Director, Dramaturg and Producer whose work has focused on giving a platform to the voices, stories and creativity of BAME and diverse communities. She is Artistic Director of Maya Productions for whom she has directed *Babel Junction* and *In Time*. She is also Artistic Associate at Soho Theatre, where she led the creative learning department for ten years and directed over fifteen new writing productions, ran its unique young writers programmes and pioneered the company's groundbreaking site specific and digital work with communities.

DAVID DUCHIN Production Manager
David has been production managing and general managing in UK theatre, live art and events since 2005. Credits include national tours with Tiata Fahodzi, People Show; London theatres include Soho Theatre, Arcola Theatre, Southwark Playhouse, Theatre503.

RHIAN KENNEDY Stage Manager
Rhian has a BA Hons in Stage Management from Rose Bruford College. Her credits include: *Port Authority* (Southwark Playhouse), *Cross Purpose* (King's Head), *Dear World* (Charing Cross Theatre) and *Candida* (Theatre Royal Bath). Other projects are: the first Manchester International Festival, Halle Orchestra's 150th Anniversary Concert and, most recently, *Twelfth* Night (New Liverpool Everyman). She also fits in work with 2.8 Hours Later (a zombie chase game) and countless cabaret and burlesque shows.

SARA RHODES-CANNING Assistant Stage Manager
After graduating over ten years ago, Sarah spent two
years as Assistant Stage Manager at Queen's Theatre
Hornchurch working on numerous shows, before moving
to Watford Palace Theatre where she spent a further
four years working on various shows, in a variety of roles.
After leaving Watford, she has worked on a number of
shows including *Yes, Prime Minister* at Trafalgar studio
1, UK tours of *Bette and Joan* and *Never Forgot*, a site-
specific piece for Headlong Theatre Company, as well as
various Pantos up and down the country including a Rock
and Roll panto at the New Wolsey, Ipswich.

MOJI BAMTEFA Costumes
Moji is a leading costume maker with 45 years of
experience. She runs voluntary organisation IJAPA,
teaching young people to make a living by making
clothes. Recent theatre: *The Estate* and 2010 Olivier Award
nominee *Iya-Ile* (Soho Theatre); *Zulu Sofola's Wedlock
of the Gods* (Cochrane Theatre); *Ola Rotimi's The Gods
Are Not to Blame* (Arcola Theatre) and *Our Husband
Has Gone Mad Again* (Broadway Barking). Recent film:
A Place Called Home, *Twins of the Rainforest*, *The White
Handkerchief* (MNET Africa) and *Saworoide* (Mainframe).

Pandora's Box National Tour Sept/Oct 2014

The Black-E, Liverpool (12 Sept)
The Lowry, Salford (13 Sept)
Newcastle Arts Centre (16 Sept)
Bradford Theatres (17 Sept)
Seven Arts, Leeds (18 Sept)
Sheffield Theatres (19-20 Sept)
The Drum, Birmingham (1 Oct)
The Hub Theatre/Mayflower Theatre, Southampton (2-4 Oct)
Millfield Arts Centre, London (8 Oct)
Carnival Arts Centre, Luton (9 Oct)
Broadway Theatre, Catford, London (10 Oct)
Broadway Theatre, Barking (23 Oct)
Bernie Grant Arts Centre, Tottenham, London (24-25 Oct)
CLF Arts Café, Bussey Building, Peckham, London (27 Oct-28 Oct)
Arcola Theatre, London (29 Oct-1 Nov)

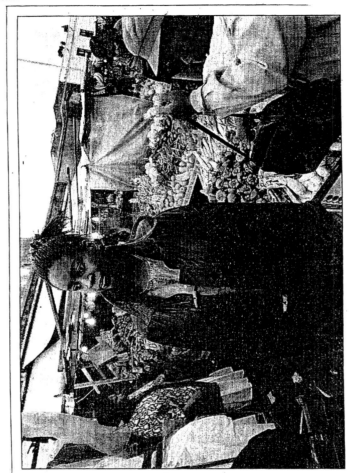

Adeola Solanke on the challenge of being 'an African abroad'

A life lived here and there

Home Front

THE ODDEST thing I learned at school was that not all children have brothers and sisters they haven't met. But in my experience, that of an African born in England, having close but geographically distant family (three elder sisters in my case) is unremarkable.

Like many of my friends ("British born", as we're classified in Nigeria), I have always felt as much a part of my parents' country as I have of England where I have always lived. Sometimes, especially after the first time I visited Nigeria as an 18-year-old in 1982, I have felt more a part of "there" than "there". The food, the clothes, the music, the customs, the sound of the Yoruba language, the ubiquitous Muslim prayers (though I'm not a Muslim) and the sheer energy zapping around in places like Lagos; all

signal "home" to me as much as a red London bus or a wet Saturday afternoon.

Growing up in London in the Sixties I distinctly remember watching TV footage of the Biafran war and listening, cross-legged, to grown-ups debating the rights and wrongs of Nigeria's civil war as though it were taking place in our very front room. To them, "there" was here and integration and assimilation were irrelevant because they were only passing through.

I imbibed part of this mentality: the borders of the British Isles have never framed my sense of national consciousness. "But you were born here, you are British," schoolfriends always insisted. Yes, I am, but I'm a Nigerian too.

My parents, both Yorubas from Western Nigeria, came to London in the Fifties to study: my father for his law degree, my mother to upgrade the midwifery certificate which she had already obtained in Nigeria. We (myself and my three sisters and one brother who were

born in London) became an inconvenient cause for them to delay their return home.

In the end we stayed for the reason they came: education outside a system which was increasingly wracked by economic, political, religious and social tensions. Today, there is a mini-exodus of young people leaving Nigeria in search of work.

I AM STILL amazed at how casually we became part of Britain — and stunned at how unprepared the system was for our presence. One Classics school textbook I was given in the sixth form informed me that Athenians were superior to modern Westerners in the same way that Europeans were superior to Africans! Information available in schools and through the media about Africa is still scant, and generally gives a negative image.

Luckily, images of a different order also get through. Pictures

from "home" would and still do arrive. Our family albums are updated with snaps of sisters, uncles, getting on with the ordinary things in life like weddings, naming ceremonies, funerals, etc. Not a famine or drought in sight.

In Nigeria I'm often seen as a Black American. People still exclaim "Are you a Nigerian?" when I mention my name after interrupting some comment about me they've carelessly made thinking I can't understand the language.

The biggest barrier is the residual colonial mentality which ascribes status to "Oyinbo" or the English. Mix that with the generally snobbish and insular attitude towards outsiders that many Africans have, and you have an instant dilemma: I find myself treated with an odd combination of disdain and deference.

At one point I felt awkward about being born abroad, especially in the company of Nigerians. I hated my accent, and my typical English reserve which stood out a

● Adeola Solanke . . . very much at home at the market in Dalston

PHOTOGRAPH: SEAN SMITH

mile amidst African spontaneity. I also didn't understand all of the social etiquette that structure relationships in Yoruba (and other African) society.

One blunder was to put out my hand to greet an elderly aunt. She kindly, but definitely, informed me that the gesture was rude coming from someone young to an elder.

Nowadays, though, I have not so much a feeling of sitting on a fence between two cultures, as grazing in either as suits my whim. I consider, myself an African abroad. What my children will make of being Africans born of Africans born abroad is another matter altogether; but Africans they will be.

Adeola Solanke is a freelance writer.

FOREWORD

Thoughts of our children's futures, especially anxieties about how they'll eventually turn out, preoccupy every parent in whatever culture or part of the world they happen to live. Toyin, the single mother and major character in Ade Solanke's delightful, thought-provoking, but ultimately reassuring play, *Pandora's Box*, is no exception.

Toyin's dilemma – about whether to leave her only child in a new school on another continent – is made all the more difficult because she's had to grapple with, and resolve for herself, issues about her own identity and her sense of home and belonging.

These are issues that lie deep in her past upbringing in the United Kingdom as a British-born child of migrant parents from Africa who are 'here' but with strong attachments to 'there'. That she in the end agrees with her family to leave her son, Rotimi, to be 'properly' educated and brought up in Nigeria, shows her pragmatism and determination to do whatever it takes, as most parents do, to reclaim, redirect and protect her son from himself, and from the dangerous slope of our British social landscape in which young African and African diasporic male children disproportionately go astray; sometimes temporarily (as teens from all cultures do), but oftentimes seriously, if not fatally.

Ade Solanke has written a very entertaining play, one which boldly takes on a very crucial issue of our time: the question of what it means to be an African diasporic parent living in the United Kingdom today and bringing up children, especially male children, in a society which, inexplicably, it seems, is constructed to make them fail. This is a play that, both in its playfulness and seriousness, manages to speak to all generations of Africans and peoples of African descent in the diaspora, now and in the future, about the emotions and anxieties in the constant traffic between here and there, between home and exile. The play is filled with characters who, in their hopes, desires, and actions, are human in every respect.

Professor Osita Okagbue
Goldsmiths, University of London, May 2012

PANDORA'S BOX: GENESIS OF A PLAY

'Are you ready to sign, Mrs Kane?' A little-known line from one of cinema's best-known films, and one of the inspirations for *Pandora's Box*.

Orson Welles' 1940s seminal work, *Citizen Kane*, looks at the consequences of a mother's choice to send her young son away. Stern, unflinching Mrs Kane decides her son will be better off educated by others. He does indeed become rich and famous, but dies an unhappy man, unable to overcome the emotional damage the early separation and uprootment caused.

The theme recurs in another well-known story, *The Fresh Prince of Bel Air*. In this popular 1990s TV sitcom, a young African-American male is relocated by his anxious mum to a more privileged environment in order to protect him from the pressures of the hood.

And it rears its head again in the story of Moses, in a biblical setting this time, when another anxious mother sends her son away to be raised by strangers, to spare him from the wholesale slaughter being inflicted on all the newborn males of her tribe.

The main character in my play, Toyin, is a descendant of these women. Like them, she's looked at the life-chances available to her son in the environment he's in and said, 'nope, not this one.'

But unlike Mrs Kane, she wobbles. She gets cold feet about her decision to send her teenage son, Timi, away from London to a new school in Nigeria. And just hours before her flight back to the UK without him, as the principal of the new school wends his way through Lagos traffic to collect her only child, she tells her family she's changed her mind.

Wahala (mayhem) ensues!

The piece was also born of observation of a trend I began to notice about six years ago.

At Lagos International Airport, in 2006, I noticed the arrivals lounge was full of kids with English accents. It was early September. Shouldn't they be in departures, I thought, on their way back to England for the start of term?

But they'd come to Nigeria FOR the start of term. They were British-born diaspora kids whose parents (mostly British-born too) were opting to educate them in Africa. Some had been plucked out of 'good' schools with prestigious reputations. Why?

'All black children should spend at least a few years of their lives in a black majority nation, for their developmental well-being,' said one parent. 'They get to see black people as prime ministers, architects, lawyers, leaders. It widens their horizons. They see alternative ways to live, and other ways to be.'

A Brixton mother was there with her five-year-old daughter, 'I'm not taking any chances,' she said. A couple from Barking told me their priest had advised them as newly-weds: primary school, London; secondary school, Nigeria.

Those encounters sparked this play, along with the many conversations with friends who, like me, have wrestled with the question: where is the best place to raise an African diaspora child in the 21st century?

Many children who are sent home go willingly and successfully. They're eager for an African experience. But what about the refuseniks? The kids who don't want to relocate, or those who are going off track and are in need of some sort of intervention to stave off disaster? Is it right for them?

Many parents were against the idea of 'transportation' for troubled kids, saying, 'you stick it out wherever you are. Deal with your child's issues yourself. Work to build and improve institutions where you live. Don't run back to Africa.'

Others claimed it was 'an admission of failure' if any parent had to send their child away. Some said cultural dislocation could lead to confusion and schizophrenia! But the majority argued that a lack of cultural identity is what ails disaffected children, and a 'dose' of the motherland is the best fix. I listened. As the headlines about teen trouble proliferated, I sniffed a great story.

Pandora's Box looks at the relative merits of London vs. Lagos re the education of British-African kids. Why should an African experience make any difference to born and bred Londoners? How and why is it that children who are failing here often come back transformed? What do they get in Africa that they don't get here? How can we give that 'thing' (a sense of self, I'd argue) to those children whose parents don't have the means to access it for them?

The play explores the universal human subject of a parent's struggle to do what's best for his/her child. But it's the first time the drama of sending a child back home to Africa has been set on the British stage. So it's also a story that has never been told before.

Why not? Because the first generation of British-born Africans is only now coming of age to tell it. These challenges are happening to us for the first time. These dilemmas are upon us here and now, as we raise our kids and try to navigate them through life, and come of age as British-born children who are now parents ourselves. And our 'coming of age' coincides with the new era of 'Africa Rising.' That too presents those of us born in the West with delicious dilemmas and juicy conflicts: here or there? Part-here, part-there? We here, kids there? Kids here, we there? Now it's time to reflect on these issues, to dramatise these choices, argue about them, write about them, and share our unique stories with the world.

I hope you enjoy the play. I loved writing it.

And I still don't know if Toyin made the right choice! What do you think?

Ade Solanke
London, May 2012

ADE SOLANKE

PANDORA'S BOX

OBERON BOOKS
LONDON

First published in 2012 by Oberon Books Ltd
521 Caledonian Road, London N7 9RH
Tel: 020 7607 3637 / Fax: 020 7607 3629
e-mail: info@oberonbooks.com
www.oberonbooks.com

A catalogue record for this book is available from the British
Library.

PB ISBN: 978-1-84943-497-3
E ISBN: 978-1-84943-599-4

Cover image by Lulu Kitololo at Asilia

Printed, bound and converted
by CPI Group (UK) Ltd, Croydon, CR0 4YY.

Visit www.oberonbooks.com to read more about all our books
and to buy them. You will also find features, author interviews and
news of any author events, and you can sign up for e-newsletters
so that you're always first to hear about our new releases.

Characters

TOYIN
A London mother (late thirties)

SIS RONKE
Her elder sister, a Lagos entrepreneur and
socialite (late thirties)

MAMA-RONKE / PANDORA
Their mother, a retired nurse (sixties)

BEV
Toyin's best friend (late thirties)

BABA
Toyin's Uncle, Mama's brother (sixties)

TIMI
Toyin's teenage son (15)

TOPE
Timi's cousin (16)

PRINCIPAL OSUN
Principal of Tope's school (fifties)

This is a one-act play. The action takes place over one
evening in late August, in Lagos, Nigeria.

NB. Dialogue is often in Nigerian-English.

SCENE ONE

Adelabu Street, Surulere, Lagos. August.

A large and opulent front room, filled with expensive furniture. The wall at the back is dominated by a large window. It's open and from the street the sounds of early evening Lagos life waft in: the traffic, the hawkers, the Fuji music. The other walls are lined with family portraits and photos, as is an elaborate oak sideboard. A clock on it says 6pm. The room is so quiet we can we hear its loud ticking.

In the middle of the room is a sturdy, if well-worn, brown trunk. It's the type generations of Africans will recognize: the one you store things in, for when you return home from abroad.

A WOMAN, TOYIN (late thirties) is kneeling before it, praying feverishly.

TOYIN: *(English accent.)* Please, God, please, please, let me be doing the right thing.

> *She stands up. We see she's attractive, well-dressed and...very, very stressed. If girlfriend slept last night, it wasn't restful! She takes a deep breath, braces herself and goes to a pile of suitcases stacked neatly by the door.*
>
> *There's one solitary case placed apart from the others; it's bright blue, whilst all the others are reds and pinks.*
>
> *She takes that case and another one from the other side. She opens the first and unloads its content. Top of the pile is a slick navy and gold school uniform. She holds it up, looks at it wistfully before tossing it aside.*

TOYIN: You HAVE made the right choice, Toyin. You're his mother.

> *Agitated, she starts sifting things from the blue case into the second one as the door opens. Another WOMAN enters. Meet ALHAJA RONKE OGUNBOLA (42), a Lagos socialite and entrepreneur. Handsome, imposing, and dressed in traditional Nigerian attire with a trendy, designer twist, she strides into the space like a tank. TOYIN swerves to avoid being barged by her heavy shopping bags.*

TOYIN: Hi...oh, look out, Sis Ronke.

SIS RONKE: *(Nigerian accent.)* Oya. Oya. Move this. Move it.

> *TOYIN shoves the suitcases aside and RONKE dumps her bags. She slumps down into a plush sofa, swiping off her headgear and kicking off her heels.*

SIS RONKE: Yea. My feet. *(Calling.)* Taofiki. TAOFIKI! That useless fool. I had to carry these from the car myself. Yet he dares to calls himself my houseboy! *(Shouting.)* Taofiki! *(Pointing to the trunk.)* Ah ah. What is that?

TOYIN: It's the box we've been waiting for. From the freight company in London? My mum *(She pauses and glances up at RONKE.)* ...I mean, our mum...is looking for the key... *(She gulps.)* ...OUR mum is looking for the right key...

SIS RONKE: Oh, 'YOUR mum' is looking for the key. Very good. *(Calling out.)* TAOFIKI. Wambi *[come here]* *(To TOYIN.)* What's inside?

TOYIN: Things she's been collecting for you. She brought them with us.

SIS RONKE: *(Snorting.)* Thirty-nine years later. TAOFIKI!

TOYIN: 'For my daughter in Nigeria, for my daughter in Nigeria'. That's all we kids in London ever heard.

SIS RONKE: Indeed. Motherly love. Ha!

She picks up a mobile phone, pounds the keys.

TOYIN: Now we're in Nigeria, she can finally give them to you.

SIS RONKE: Wonderful. How nice of her. *(She barks into the phone.)* Ah ah. How long do you want me to wait? Tell the driver to bring the rest of the bags up. *(She hangs up.)* That Taofiki. When I see him, he will suffer for this. So, where is YOUR Mum?

Another WOMAN enters, also wearing traditional dress. This is their mother, MRS PANDORA OLADURO (65), a stout and kindly woman. She's jangling a bunch of keys. As per Yoruba culture, she's addressed by the name of her eldest, Ronke.

MAMA-RONKE: I was right. They were in the red suitcase, under the fabric. Oh, Ronke, my dear, you're back.

RONKE: Yes, Ma'mi. *(She gets up a little grudgingly, and curtsies, as the YORUBA do to any elder.)* Good evening, ma.

MAMA-RONKE: Welcome back. How was the drive?

RONKE: We didn't get there till 5. Baba was so hungry.

MAMA-RONKE: I told him to eat before he left. Two hours from Surulere to Yaba! Lagos!

RONKE: Because of the political rally. Here. I picked up the shea butter and chewing sticks for Auntie Joy. *(She holds out two paper bags.)*

MAMA-RONKE: *(Taking them.)* Ah, she'll appreciate it. The real thing, direct from Africa.

She heads to the cases, then stops.

MAMA-RONKE: No, I'd better pack this in my hand luggage.

She turns to leave, now spotting TOYIN's pile of unfolded clothes.

MAMA-RONKE: Hey! Toyin, you still haven't packed Rotimi's case? What have you been doing? Ah ah. *(She picks it up.)* Why is his uniform for the new school on the floor?

TOYIN: Mum, I've got something to tell you… I've decided…

MAMA-RONKE: *(Dusting it down.)* The Principal is coming to collect him in… *(She glances at the clock.)* yeh! Six o'clock!…at seven…in less than an hour. And we still have to unload this trunk. Is something the matter with you?

MAMA-RONKE puts the uniform back into the blue suitcase.

TOYIN: Mum, listen, I have to tell you…

MAMA-RONKE: Na you sabi. Carry on wasting time. I'm not going to let you make me miss my flight. *(She goes to the trunk and fiddles with the lock.)* Ronke?

SIS RONKE: Ma'mi?

MAMA-RONKE: *(Re. key.)* Olorun! What kind of wahala is this? Where can that useless key be, for goodness' sake? Ronke?

SIS RONKE: Yes, I answered you, ma.

MAMA-RONKE: The driver can start loading the cases in my room. I'm not risking this your Lagos traffic. We must leave as soon as the Principal collects Timi.

TOYIN flinches at those words, stomps over to TIMI's case, grabs the uniform and dumps it on the floor again, firmly. Her mother notices and turns to her quick-sharp.

MAMA-RONKE: What? Because of what Baba said?

As RONKE looks on, she grasps TOYIN's hand, tenderly.

MAMA-RONKE: My dear, Baba means well. But we know better. Timi will be better off in Africa.

RONKE studies their closeness as TOYIN takes a deep breath, about to bite the bullet.

TOYIN: No, Mum, I've got something to tell you…

MAMA-RONKE: Come on, don't be silly. The time for talking is over. Now, those keys…

TOYIN: Mum, listen, I can't…

MAMA-RONKE: No more nonsense. Please!

MAMA exits. She's not hearing this.

TOYIN: Mum…

TOYIN follows her, but, catching RONKE's silent glare, she stops, perplexed.

TOYIN: What? *(Searching her memory for what she's done wrong now.)* Oh, I'm sorry. Yeah, I know, I did it again, didn't I?… I meant our mum, not MY mum.

SIS RONKE: *(Riled in a way even she doesn't quite understand.)* Don't be sorry. It's what you are. It's not your fault. You and your son. That boy…

TOYIN: I beg your pardon. His name is Timi.

SIS RONKE: Whatever you call him. You're both the same. E ni e ko. No manners. He still refuses to prostrate to his elders. And today, again, he addressed me as Ronke. I told you to tell him: in Africa, children don't call adults by their first name…

TOYIN: I've told him, Ronke…

SIS RONKE: See. See! Look at that. Even for you – my junior sister – to call me by my first name is rude. Like mother, like son. London people. No manners. No respect.

Just then, there's a loud thud, thudding sound and in walks ROTIMI (15) or TIMI as he's known, TOYIN's son. He's bouncing a football and wears jeans, an Arsenal football shirt and NY hat. His skin and eyes gleam – result of years of MAMA's pounded yam and okra stew. He's cool, slick and super-confident. A manchild rushing to mannishness. Butter wouldn't melt in his mouth. Would it?

TIMI: What's popping, peeps?

SIS RONKE: Peeps, ke! E ma wo omo yii *[Look at this child]*. Are we your age-mates?

TOYIN: Darling, don't bounce the ball in here.

TIMI: *(Still bouncing it.)* Mum, I need some more money. They've got another Lil-Wayne T-shirt in that shop across the road. Hi, Ronke.

SIS RONKE: *(Spluttering.)* What?

TIMI: It's chee-eap, man. Mum, mum quick. 2,000 naira. That's like – only eight pounds. Hey, what you doing with my suitcase?

TOYIN: Timi, remember what I said about how you address your elders.

TIMI: Oh, yeah, yeah, yeah. Sorry, sorry, sorry. Actually, mum, they had this hat too. Make it 4,000?

SIS RONKE: Your mother is speaking to you and you're asking her for money. Not even saying please!

TOYIN: TIMI?

TIMI: Sorry, *(Rolling his eyes.)* AUNTIE Ronke. The money, Mum? PLEASE.

He gets her bag and hands it to her, rubbing his hands in anticipation as she fishes out her purse and counts out the money. He dips in and takes a few extra notes.

TIMI: Cheers, love.

SIS RONKE: Love!

TOYIN: Wait. Did you put on insect repellent before you went out?

TIMI: Yep.

TOYIN: Are you sure?

TIMI: *(Irritated.)* Yeeees!

TOYIN: Wait. I don't want you to get malaria.

She takes a tube of cream out of her bag, opens it and starts rubbing some on his legs. He wriggles and squirms.

TIMI: Stop it!

SIS RONKE: *(Shaking her head.)* Ni to olorun! *[OMG!]* Is he a baby?

TIMI: That's enough! *(Fiercely now.)* Leave me alone, mum!

TOYIN: OK, I just want to…

TIMI: I said no, didn't I?

He escapes and exits, bouncing the ball. TOYIN is a little shaken by his vehemence.

SIS RONKE: Doormat of the year! No wonder he's as he is. And he thinks he can treat everyone else the same way. Well, he will see. Next time he calls me by name, I will slap his face. Write it on the wall.

TOYIN: What?

SIS RONKE: I said, next time he dares calls me by name...

TOYIN: I don't think so. Don't talk – don't you even dare think – about touching my child.

SIS RONKE: Indeed? And what are you going to do about it?

TOYIN: *(Riled.)* You slap my son and I'll slap you!

SIS RONKE: You said what!!!

TOYIN: I said, you hit him and I'll hit you. Did you hear OK this time?

SIS RONKE: You'll do what...are you ill?

TOYIN: I'm not in the mood for any more of your crap. One whole month I've put up with you, because I'm a guest in your house. But I've got a lot to deal with tonight, and if you dare touch my child, you'll be sorry. I AM from London. And, trust me, I can switch.

SIS RONKE: You are threatening me? How dare you? *(She starts hurling invectives in YORUBA.)* Ori re o dara! Olori burukuu! Ori e baje... *[Your head is not good, your head is bad etc.]*

Into the storm, MAMA-RONKE re-enters, jangling another bunch of keys.

MAMA-RONKE: I think these are the ones... Ah ah. You two again!

TOYIN: *(As RONKE's tirade continues.)* Yeah, yeah, yeah. Say what you like. I can't understand your language, anyway.

MAMA-RONKE: What is it now? Ronke, don't say things like that.

TOYIN: She's trying to bully me again.

MAMA-RONKE: And you, Toyin, shut up.

TOYIN: Why should I shut up for her!

MAMA-RONKE: Because she is your senior sister. *(Turning.)* And, Ronke, this is your aburo. Your junior sister. You should be the one to set a good example.

SIS RONKE: My sister koo! My sister ni. *[Whatever!]*

TOYIN: See, I told you, Mum.

SIS RONKE: *(Mimicking her accent.)* See, I told you, mum.

TOYIN: You're just jealous.

SIS RONKE: Eh hen! Because you grew up in London? A second-class citizen of an undeveloping nation! Are you insane?

MAMA-RONKE: OK, OK. Please, the both of you! Please. Please! For my sake. Do you want to kill me!

TOYIN: She may be able to guilt-trip you, but I'm not having it. I'm sorry. Hit my son!

MAMA-RONKE: Ah, ah! What is all this about?

SIS RONKE: She threatened me. In my own home.

TOYIN: SHE threatened to hit Timi.

SIS RONKE: Fool! You should be the one to discipline him yourself. That boy is rude. Rude and unruly. Mannerless beast. He needs severe disciplining. *(Turning away.)* Like mother, like son. Anyway, when he gets to the Academy, they'll deal with him well, well.

MAMA-RONKE: I don't know who is doing this to create war between you. You are from the same mother and the same father, so why all this wahala? Please, Toyin, finish Timi's packing. The car is coming to collect him...

TOYIN: No! It's not collecting him.

MAMA-RONKE: What do you mean?

TOYIN: That's what I've been trying to tell you. I changed my mind. I'm taking him back to London.

MAMA-RONKE: Oh, come on. It's too late to change your mind again...

TOYIN looks defiant. MAMA looks around, clocking the shifted cases and finally clicking.

MAMA-RONKE: Is that why you're unpacking...? Jesu...no, no, no, no! Toyin! You can't do this.

TOYIN: Yes I can.

MAMA-RONKE: But now we've paid! £18,000 for the entire two years. Yesterday. We paid. I used all of my savings.

TOYIN: I know, mum, and I'm sorry. And I'll pay you back. Get an evening job. Whatever. But I tossed and turned all night and I've made my decision...

SIS RONKE: After all my efforts, pulling strings for him…do you think it's easy to get a place in such a top school in this Lagos…?

MAMA-RONKE: Ronke, it is enough! Please. Please, I am your mother… Toyin, listen…

SIS RONKE: As usual you take her side. Well, *(Pointing to a photo.)* THAT is my mother, the woman who raised me. Your mother. After YOU went to London and never came back.

MAMA-RONKE is chilled, so wounded.

MAMA-RONKE: *(Shaken.)* Ronke. Ronke, please. You don't mean it.

RONKE sweeps out.

TOYIN: Mum, she does mean it.

MAMA-RONKE: *(Going after RONKE.)* It's my fault. I should never have left her.

TOYIN: No. No. But you did.

Alone again, she closes her eyes and pauses, gathering her energy. She exhales deeply, opens them and starts packing again, with renewed conviction, as another woman enters. This is BEV ALEXANDER (late thirties), her best friend from London. BEV's bright and ebullient, and wearing a trendy Nigerian designer outfit. She's waving a magazine, Ovation, a Nigerian Hello-type thing.

BEV: Hiya.

TOYIN: *(Distractedly.)* Hi, hi, Bev?

BEV: Look, then.

TOYIN: *(Looking up.)* Oh, girl, you did your hair! It's nice. Anyway, listen…

BEV: Went to those Togolese girls in the salon near the roundabout. Have you seen this?

She holds out the magazine. TOYIN ignores it.

TOYIN: Bev, listen up…

BEV: Look. *(Rubbing.)* Ouch! My scalp's throbbing, but £30 for all these tiny braids…it can throb all night. Gotta look right for the book launch tonight! The governor of the Central Bank of Nigeria's going to be there…

TOYIN: Girl, listen: there's been a big change of plan…

BEV: *(Re. mag.)* Look! Your sister! On the cover. Society Woman of the Year.

TOYIN: I couldn't care less. Will you please listen …

BEV: You didn't tell me she was chair of the Lagos Chamber of Commerce.

TOYIN: Look, Bev…

BEV: Her telecoms company is one of the top ones in West Africa. Just look at this profile. LOOK!!!

BEV thrusts it under her nose. TOYIN snatches it and looks.

TOYIN: That green doesn't even suit her.

BEV: That's a Roberto Cavalli dress. And those, my dear, are real emeralds!

TOYIN*: (Reading.)* She wasn't born in Lagos, she was born in Ibadan. She's such a flipping liar. She's not a born Lagotian! And she didn't go to Queens' College. She went to a Federal Boarding School. My mum was always going on about having to pay her fees 'at Federal Boarding School.'

BEV: Well, girl, you and I didn't go to any school like that. Our Lady's School for Girls was not fee-paying. *(Reading over TOYIN's shoulder.)* Look, a first in Business Studies from Lagos University. And her husband's law firm is the top one in Lagos. That's like a Magic Circle law firm in London.

TOYIN: *(Tossing it away.)* Yeah, so what? What kind of person is she? Look how she treats her servants.

BEV: I just saw Taofiki in the mai-guard's hut. Is he hiding again?

TOYIN: After the way she hit him this morning! He's too scared to come in. Just for dropping a pot of soup!

BEV: She is a bit stroppy. He's just a child. She shouldn't bully him like that.

TOYIN: He's the same age as Timi. Look at all this. Lovely home. Nannies for her children, one each! Cooks, driver…

BEV: She's got it all.

TOYIN: But she's still not satisfied.

BEV: Just imagine: no shopping, no laundry, no cooking… Dapo says we'll have a houseboy and a housegirl…

TOYIN: *(Covering her ears and moving away.)* Look, I do not want to hear any more about Dapo. I've got important news…

BEV: And you know I'll need a driver. Frankly, the way they drive…

TOYIN: Bev, have you finished packing? 'Cos you do know our flight leaves at midnight?

BEV: He says it's love. I think he means it.

TOYIN: Yeah, he's in love alright. With your passport.

BEV: Oh, come on.

TOYIN: It's all about the British passport. The red P. He thinks you're some stupid Jammo he can use to get to London and then dump.

BEV: He'd never use that derogatory term. And I'm Antiguan, not Jamaican.

TOYIN: *(Shaking her head.)* You've only known him a month and you're dropping your whole life? It's crazy.

BEV: What's crazy? Beverly Alexander trying something new and Social Services grinds to a halt? Meals on wheels can manage without me! If you want to sit in that grubby office on that grimy high street for the rest of your life, good luck to you. I'll send postcards for you, Darren, Sonia and the others to stick on the canteen noticeboard. You're the crazy one – going back. You said you were sick of London too.

TOYIN: Yeah, I know. I know. I am, but…nowhere's perfect and…well, it's home.

BEV: So? Our parents left THEIR homes. They picked up and left. Why can't we? Do something different? Experience pastures NEW? Lagos is like…like…Toyin, I don't care how much you all laugh at me, but it's true: every day here I feel more and more at home. I just get this sense that I've been here before. It's like déjà vu. I'm back! And it's so exciting. *(Re. mag.)* People are achieving, they're ambitious, they're happy…if you work hard, the sky's the limit…no concrete ceiling. You better believe I'm staying. What's wrong with that? If I change my mind, London isn't going anywhere.

TOYIN: Bev, go and pack.

BEV: I'm not marrying him. Yet! Anyway, do I have anything left TO pack?

TOYIN: Oh no! They didn't?

BEV: Yep. They did.

TOYIN: What did I say? I warned you about my nieces.

BEV: Like a swarm of locusts. Talk about military precision. Funke went for the clothes, Temi pounced on the jewellery. The whole operation only took five minutes. Look. *(Pointing to her feet.)* Flip-flops. Shoes gone clear!

TOYIN: I bet that was Yinka.

BEV: And she's not even the same shoe size!

TOYIN: They're so greedy.

BEV: Anyway, they have been teaching me Yoruba. Sho'g bo *[Pronounced: sho og boh]?* That means 'do you understand?' for PEOPLE who haven't even BOTHERED learning any Yoruba since they've been here…hint, hint…

TOYIN: Please! Anyway, listen up, change of plan…

BEV: Dapo's different, Toyin. There's something about him…the culture, all the men here…they're…different…come on, you know what I'm talking about. Be honest. That's why you're leaving Timi.

TOYIN: *(Snapping.)* Look, for god's sake, Bev. You're not staying and I'm not leaving Timi. OK?

BEV: What?

TOYIN: What I just said: he's not staying. I'm taking him back to London.

BEV: Come off it, Toyin.

TOYIN: What? Leave my baby here? Alone? I must have been nuts.

BEV: He won't be alone. He'll be at a fantastic boarding school. With Tope and lots of other kids, from here and from all over the world.

TOYIN: I don't know what possessed me! Nuts!

BEV: But what about the fees? You've already paid now.

TOYIN: Because you and mum dragged me there. I told you I was having second thoughts.

BEV sits down, serious now.

BEV: OK, let's go over it all again…

TOYIN: No. No, not this time.

BEV: This isn't easy. I understand that. But you've come this far…

TOYIN: *(Covering her ears.)* You're not talking me round again.

BEV: But you were the one…a new start for him. It was all your idea.

TOYIN: After YOU got the application forms from Tope's mum.

BEV: But it was what you wanted. For Timi's future, you kept saying.

TOYIN: None of it was my idea. I just let myself get swept along…bullied…

BEV: You went along with it because you know.

TOYIN: There is nothing wrong with my son!

BEV: Don't give up now, Toyin. A few more hours and you're home and dry. You've found a great school, you've got him a place…

She grabs TOYIN and pulls her to the front window.

BEV: Look out there. What do you see? People, right? Just people. Because there are no 'black' people in Africa. Let him have that for a change. Let him grow, develop, succeed.

TOYIN: *(Turning away.)* Succeed? Materially, maybe. How will he feel? Will he be happy? Will he fit in?

BEV: Please! So people they tease us about our accents. Big deal.

TOYIN: They call us 'Oyinbo dudu.' 'Black white people!'

BEV: So? We've been called worse in England! Who cares?

TOYIN: At the art gallery yesterday, when I was buying that carving, my cousin nudged me and said 'look, some people like you.' When I turned round and looked, guess what he was pointing at?

BEV: What?

TOYIN: Some German tourists.

BEV: What does he know!

TOYIN: He wasn't being cruel. He was just stating a fact. To him, we're foreigners. And in my heart, I've never been sure about leaving Timi. Let's face it. I don't really know my family here, not really. Neither does he.

BEV: They're still family.

TOYIN: Like my 'sister' Ronke! Please. You really overestimate this me being African stuff. Just because we have African names and relatives…that doesn't mean that we belong. Or that they accept us.

BEV: Well, it's more than I've got. He's got his name, his tribe…

TOYIN: Oh, Bev, do not let that fool Dapo rename you!

BEV: I'm not changing my name. It reflects my history. I'm just saying Timi belongs here. This is his home, Toyin, his motherland.

TOYIN: But he won't have me, his mother.

She snaps shut the suitcase and takes it to the door. She picks up some luggage labels and writes on them. BEV weighs up whether to speak. She takes the plunge.

BEV: Well, maybe at this stage that'll be good for him. You can be a little…over-indulgent…and he can get a little out of hand… I'm saying this with love…

TOYIN: All kids get into trouble sometimes. And anyway, you wouldn't understand. You're not a mother.

BEV: Excuse me!

This is TOYIN's trump card. BEV is pricked but TOYIN is unrepentant. BEV's about to retort when MAMA-RONKE comes in, weary as hell.

MAMA-RONKE: Toyin, we have to talk about your decision… Oh, Bev, you're back. Ah, so that's where you went.

BEV: Hello, Aunty Pandora. Like it?

MAMA-RONKE: Oh, it's nice. How much did you pay?

BEV: Eight thousand naira.

MAMA-RONKE: They robbed you! Just because you're a foreigner…what's this?

She picks up the magazine.

BEV: What should I have paid?

MAMA-RONKE: Four thousand at most.

BEV: No!

MAMA-RONKE: Oh, look at Ronke.

BEV: She's in the centre pages too. Eight pages on her and her fundraising ball for Orphans International. *(Turning to TOYIN.)* This is how people can succeed in Nigeria.

MAMA-RONKE: *(Taking the mag and sitting down.)* She married well. Her business is doing well. At least my mother's efforts were not in vain.

TOYIN: And your efforts. You were always sending money 'home.' Even though we never had any in London.

MAMA-RONKE: *(Flicking through.)* Olodumare! My life.

TOYIN: *(Joining her.)* That's a nice one, I suppose. At least she's smiling.

BEV: *(Squeezing in.)* Which one? Oh, yeah.

TOYIN: My big sister. She looked so sweet in the photo album. Never thought being with her would be like this.

MAMA-RONKE: Those were taken the day I left Nigeria.

TOYIN: She looked so sweet and sad.

MAMA-RONKE: She was crying at the docks. I nearly turned back. But I told myself, Pandora, go to England and do your studies. When you qualify, you'll come back and be able to do even more for her.

TOYIN: Mum, what's done is done. You didn't plan to stay in England.

MAMA-RONKE: I've tried so hard to talk to her, to explain. But she won't listen. Just now she refused to let me into her room. Told me to go away, to leave her and 'go to London, just like you did when I was a baby.' Yes, that is what she just said.

BEV: Oh, purleez! She's a grown woman. Aunty Pandora, She's just guilt-tripping you.

MAMA-RONKE: But she was just a baby. How could I have done such a thing?

TOYIN: It's a power trip. You just have to stand up to her.

Just then, the lights flash on and off and suddenly, we're plunged into darkness.

MAMA-RONKE: NEPA!

BEV: Oh my god, not again!

TOYIN: That's the 'motherland' for you, Bev.

She picks up a kerosene lamp and puts it on the table. BEV strikes a match and lights it. Its gentle glow fills the darkness. They watch the flame a moment.

BEV: It is better to light a candle than to curse the darkness.

TOYIN: Your mum always said that.

MAMA-RONKE: Toyin, I know you think Ronke is harsh. But she's been through a lot. She wasn't even three years old when I left. I was so excited – to win a scholarship, to travel overseas, to be going to London at last! But I couldn't do my nursing training and look after her at the same time. So I left her behind, because I thought she'd have a better life.

TOYIN: She did. You left her with granny. And Baba. She had all of them spoiling her. He told me himself. They loved her like she was you.

MAMA-RONKE: But without her mother? Maybe she felt abandoned? Rejected? And, look, now she rejects me.

BEV: You didn't abandon her. You left her for the right reasons. *(To TOYIN.)* Like any good mother would. Like my mum did with my brothers in Antigua. And it's not like you were partying. You were studying AND working and sending money back. Wasn't it hard for you too, living without her?

MAMA-RONKE: Ah! Of course. My first born.

BEV: See.

MAMA-RONKE: I tried my best, but maybe leaving her was a mistake. I don't know anymore!

TOYIN: Exactly! And you want me to…

MAMA-RONKE: But you, Toyin, your own is different. YOU have no choice. Timi is a good boy, but in London he's not safe. You saw what happened to Rio? Shot and killed on his doorstep. You know what happened to Samuel? Stabbed for his phone.

BEV: I can't read the Gazette anymore. It's too depressing!

MAMA-RONKE: It's affecting Timi. Affecting him very deeply. He's changed in the last year.

BEV: Especially since Rio. He's been…different.

TOYIN: Well, his best friend killed. 'Course he's sad.

BEV: He's hardened.

TOYIN: He's not in any trouble.

MAMA-RONKE: Do you know what he's doing when he's outside? Toyin, my dear, I can only tell you what I know. That boy is your only son. He's no longer a child. He'll soon turn sixteen and you won't have any more say in his life.

This is your last chance. I am your mother and I advise you, I beg you…

She's about to get down on her knees, but Toyin stops her, horrified. For a parent to kneel to a child is a taboo.

TOYIN: Mum, no!

MAMA-RONKE: When Principal Osun comes, sign the papers, if you really want that boy to ever amount to anything in life.

BEV: Toyin, your mother is on her knees.

TOYIN: Mum, get up.

MAMA-RONKE: Please, my dear, don't let what happened to your brothers happen to him. My only grandson, don't let another generation be lost in that land. I've tried so hard to help you, after you ended up on your own. Now, after all my sacrifices…

TOYIN: Mum, please get up. Please…

Just then, TIMI comes back into the semi-dark room.

TIMI: No electricity again, man. Nigeria is a joke.

The lights come back on and now we see he's wearing the new T-shirt, a new hat and carrying a pineapple. He hands it to TOYIN.

TIMI: Here, Mum. This is from the lady you bought one from yesterday.

TOYIN: Thank you, baby.

BEV: Aah, sweet. Hi, babes.

TIMI: *(Giving her a quick peck on the cheek.)* Always sweet, Aunt Bev. You know me. Hi, granny. *(Kissing her too.)* Are you crying, granny?

MAMA-RONKE: No, no. Hello, hello, my wonderful.

TIMI: What were you talking about just now?

TOYIN: Nothing, love.

TIMI: You're planning something for my birthday! My Super Sweet 16th. Just tell me.

BEV: It's a surprise.

TIMI: Guess what? I went on an 'okada'

TOYIN: Not one of those motorbikes?

TIMI: Yep. A red and silver one.

TOYIN: Timi, I told you not to. You could have fallen off!

BEV: Leave him alone. He's not a baby!

TOYIN: But it's dangerous. You could have been hurt.

BEV: You're no stranger to danger, are you, Timi?

> *She tries to grab him as he passes. He dodges nimbly, trying to look nonchalant.*

TIMI: I'm a lover, Auntie Bev, not a fighter.

MAMA-RONKE: How was the football?

TIMI: I scored three. They got some wicked players here, man. And you know Obi Mikel? The Chelsea midfielder? He used to train at that pitch. But guess what? They haven't even got real goalposts. And most of them ain't even got boots! But they're proper good.

MAMA-RONKE: Of course! We're Africans. We always excel. We work hard and success follows.

TIMI: Yeah, granny. But I'm a hustler, you get me?

BEV: Which part of you is a hustler?

TIMI: I'm hustler and I'm a pimp, Auntie Bev *(Singing.)* 'I'm a hustler, a hustler...'

> *The others look pointedly at TOYIN who avoids their gaze.*

BEV: A hustler you say?

> *She looks at TOYIN pointedly, who thrusts labels at her.*

TOYIN: Help me put these on. Timi, what do you mean you're a hustler?

TIMI: It's a song. Just joking, mum.

TOYIN: It's not funny. I want you to be a decent man. Not a hustler.

TIMI: It's just a song!

MAMA-RONKE: You better see things clearly, Toyin.

TIMI: What's in that trunk?

MAMA-RONKE: *(Leaping up.)* Yea! The trunk. Help me find the key, Bev.

> *They exit. TIMI starts fiddling with the trunk lock.*

TOYIN: *(To TIMI.)* Remember what I said: don't call my sister by her first name. Or anyone older than you. It's Aunty or Uncle. And leave that lock alone.

TIMI: What for? They're not all my aunts and uncles.

TOYIN: Never mind that. It's the custom. *(Re. lock.)* I said, leave it alone. You'll break it! You heard me. And you know you're expected to prostrate for elders.

TIMI: I don't wanna roll on the floor. It's dirty.

TOYIN: It's a mark of respect. If you don't do it, you're disgracing me.

TIMI looks at her for a moment, finally moving away from the trunk.

TIMI: But you don't kneel to granny. If you don't do it, why should I?

TOYIN: Lord Jesus! Why can't you just do as you're told? Stop questioning everything I say! That's why I have to worry about you.

TIMI: It's my opinion. You said I should always speak up with my own opinion…

TOYIN: Look, I'm fighting your corner. People say things about you, Timi, but I don't listen and I don't let them poison my mind. They don't know you like I do.

TIMI: What you on about?

TOYIN takes his hands.

TOYIN: Everyone, everything. Everywhere. Newspapers, the tv. The way they show you…

TIMI: Me? On the news?

TOYIN: I mean all of you. Young black men.

TIMI: Oh mum, not all that racism stuff again.

TOYIN: The mugshots, the headlines…plastered everywhere. I don't let any of it in. I'm still on your side… I promised I'd stand by you after your dad left, didn't I? And I have, haven't I?

TIMI: Yeah, yeah.

TOYIN: You know I'll never abandon you. It's always been you and me, hasn't it? I've always backed you up, haven't I? That's because I love you. You're my best boy, you know that, don't you?

TIMI: I'm your only boy.

TOYIN: *(Kissing, clasping him.)* You're my best, my only boy.

TIMI: And I can make your cup of tea better than anybody.

TOYIN: Better than anybody else in the whole wide world. Everything's going to be fine. I won't let anything happen to you. Trust me.

TIMI: Basically, Mum, I don't know what you're on about…

BEV re-enters, but they don't see her at first.

TOYIN: Now it's time to prove me right. You've got to pull your socks up. Timi? Timi listen. Prove me right. Be the talented and responsible young man I know you can be. OK? I believe in you. Don't let what they say come true.

TIMI: OK, OK, OK. God, man!

TOYIN: Now, go and bring all your stuff here.

TIMI: Allow it, man. Who keeps moving my case? *(Picking up the uniform.)* And what's this?

TOYIN: Leave that alone. All your stuff. Here. Now. Then shower, eat and airport.

TIMI looks at the uniform, drops it and exits.

TOYIN: *(Calling out.)* And pull your trousers up.

BEV looks at TOYIN quizzically.

BEV: You still haven't told him he's staying?

TOYIN: Just as well, since he's not.

BEV: Your mum's paid all that money. £18,000. You've come all this way and now…look, Toyin, be real. He's not the innocent little boy you think he is. I've told you – I've seen some of his new friends. I know them. I've got some of them on my caseload. They are troubled kids.

TOYIN: He's my son. I think I know him better than anyone.

BEV: *(Mimicking TIMI.)* 'I'm a hustler and a pimp.'

TOYIN bites her lip and looks down.

BEV: From top of the class to just three GCSEs! Three!

TOYIN: He got one A.

BEV: In Design and Technology! *(Quoting from the Damien Marley song, Jam Rock.)* 'Come on let's face it, a ghetto education's basic, and that's why the youths them waste it, And when they waste it, that's when they take the guns replace it, then they don't stand a chance at all.'

TOYIN: He just needs to find something he enjoys…

BEV: Timi has issues, Toyin. He did get caught with those stolen mobile phones…

TOYIN: It wasn't him.

BEV: But you storm into the headmaster's office and get him off the hook. The other two boys were excluded.

TOYIN: He told me what happened and I believe him.

BEV: Like they say, denial is not just a river in Egypt.

TOYIN: Guess what, I support my son. That's what a mother is supposed to do!

BEV: That's being a good mum: giving him what he wants, not what he needs?

TOYIN: *(Getting up.)* With all due respect, Bev, what do you know about motherhood?

BEV: Why do you always throw that in my face? I'm trying to help.

TOYIN: We don't need 'help.' My Timi is a good boy. I know he is.

End of scene one.

SCENE TWO

The same room. The clock says 8pm.

TIMI's on the Playstation. SIS RONKE is arranging more suitcases. They're all neatly labelled to go. TIMI's blue case is in the pile.

SIS RONKE: What did Tope say?

TIMI: There's a go-slow. What's that?

SIS RONKE: A traffic jam. So where are they now?

TIMI: Near the stadium. Heading for Aliharah Mashup or summink.

SIS RONKE: Alhaji Masha?

TIMI: Yeah, yeah. That's the one.

SIS RONKE: They'll be here in about ten minutes. But something so simple. Can't you even try to say it properly? Or are you totally Oyinbo? Masha. Alhaji Masha. Try now.

TIMI: Yeah, that's alright, but thanks for that.

SIS RONKE: It's the roundabout at the end of our street. You pass it every day when you go to the internet café.

TIMI: Oh yeah, I thought it sounded familiar.

TOYIN enters, carrying a tray with spuds and a knife.

TOYIN: Timi, time to take your malaria tablet. Here.

TIMI: But we're leaving tonight.

TOYIN: We have to take them for a week after we leave. Oh, I forgot the water. Go get some.

TIMI: OK.

SIS RONKE: Where's Bev?

TOYIN: She went to get a refund from the hairdressers.

SIS RONKE: *(Laughing.)* You don't get refunds in Nigeria!

TOYIN: You don't know her.

SIS RONKE: Why potatoes? The jollof is ready.

TOYIN: He wants chips. Go and get some water, Timi.

SIS RONKE: Let him eat jollof, now?

TIMI: That rice is too peppery.

TOYIN: Why can't he have what he likes? Timi, go.

TIMI still doesn't move. She puts the tray down and exits.

SIS RONKE: Mr Fish and Chips! Why aren't you interested in anything about Nigeria? It's your country, you know.

TIMI: Nah, you're alright. I'm happy with London. But thanks a lot. Very kind of you.

SIS RONKE: You are lost! Ah. O ma se o! It's a pity your mother changed her mind.

TIMI: Changed her mind about what?

SIS RONKE: Anyway, sha, there are many like you.

TOYIN re-enters with the water. She hands it to him with the tablet. He turns his head and opens his mouth. She pops the tablet in, then tilts the glass to his mouth. He guzzles both down, still on the game. SIS RONKE shakes her head in disgust.

TOYIN sits with the tray as MAMA-RONKE enters.

MAMA-RONKE: Ronke, remember I wanted to talk to you.

SIS RONKE: Yes, Ma'mi. I know.

MAMA-RONKE: What if we do it now?

SIS RONKE: But the Principal is due any moment. He's just phoned to say they're almost here.

MAMA-RONKE: It won't take long. You know I'm leaving in a few hours. We have things to discuss. It's time we…

SIS RONKE: Yes, ma. But I don't want him to interrupt us. When he leaves…

We hear a doorbell ring. MAMA sighs, resigned.

SIS RONKE: See. *(Shouting.)* Taofiki! Eti e di ni? *[Are you deaf]* Are you deaf? Open the door!

She turns to TOYIN.

SIS RONKE: By the way, you're the one who's going to tell him. It's your wahala, not mine…and don't expect your money back.

TOYIN: OK, OK. *(Nudging her.)* Sssshh.

TIMI: Tell who what?

They ignore him.

TIMI: Don't bother answering me. I'm just a kid.

SIS RONKE: I'm already embarrassed by the whole situation. After all my efforts.

TOYIN wrings her hands.

TOYIN: Timi, you better go have your wash before we eat.

TIMI: I don't need to shower…

TOYIN: *(Grabbing the Playstation control.)* Go and do it now.

TIMI: OK, OK. Take a chill pill.

> *He saunters out. TOYIN catches MAMA-RONKE and SIS RONKE exchange glances. MAMA-RONKE pulls herself up.*

MAMA-RONKE: Wo, I still haven't found those useless keys! O jare, this is too much for me.

> *As she gets up, a MAN enters hurriedly. This is BABA (67), MAMA-RONKE's elder brother. He is a tall, dark, serious man, very dignified. A really solid person.*

SIS RONKE: *(Surprised.)* BABA! You're back? We thought it was the Princi…

BABA: Good! So she hasn't signed yet…

> *TOYIN brightens at the sight of BABA. An ally, at last.*

TOYIN: Oh, uncle.

SIS RONKE: So, you mean I drove you all the way home for you to turn around and come back?

BABA: I had to come back. This is very, very important.

SIS RONKE: How did you get here? Is Dele back?

BABA: Do I need a driver to move around? I drove myself.

SIS RONKE: And you found somewhere to park? At this time?

BABA: I parked outside the church.

SIS RONKE: *(Going to the front window and peeking out.)* Evening service is starting. And tonight is their all-night vigil. They'll block you in.

MAMA-RONKE: Brother, please, no more horror stories.

BABA: Uh, uh, uh. I am the head of this family and I must speak!

MAMA-RONKE/SIS RONKE: We know. And you've already spoken!

BABA: As your elder brother and as your uncle…

> *MAMA and SIS RONKE throw up their hands. Here we go…*

MAMA-RONKE/SIS RONKE: Baba, we know your position!

BABA: Therefore, you know it is my duty to speak. You cannot silence me…you cannot censor me! You must not!

TOYIN: You've all had your say. Let uncle speak.

BABA: Toyin, when I arrived home, I changed into my house clothes, I put on my slippers and sat down to dinner. I was about to eat my eko when the lights went off.

MAMA-RONKE: Yes. And then what?

SIS RONKE: It happened here too. Is it the first time?

BABA: When the lights went off, it was as though, suddenly, a light went on inside of me.

MAMA-RONKE: Visions and dreams. As usual.

BABA: *(Shooting her a dirty look.)* A clear, bright light. A strong, tremendously powerful feeling, overtook me. I had to push the tray away and listen to the message. It was like, yes, a vision. Then, I knew, I had to come and speak again.

MAMA-RONKE: Broda, please. You don't understand London…

BABA: What don't I understand? We read the news. We have internet. We know about Damilola. And, if you don't know, we have gangs here too.

MAMA-RONKE: Not in that school.

BABA: That is true.

SIS RONKE: You've already told us what's wrong with Nigeria, you've told us what's wrong with the school…

BABA: *(To TOYIN.)* But there's something else I've now sensed. Something deeper. What is wrong about this whole situation… I had a glimmer of it in my vision… I'll soon put my finger on exactly what it is.

MAMA-RONKE: What more is there to tell us? We too read the newspapers. We have internet. We know about Nigeria.

BABA: Exactly! And you are not staying. You *(Pointing to TOYIN.)* are not staying. So, why should you leave that poor boy here? Don't you know our people are running away as fast as they can?

SIS RONKE: Exaggeration! People are returning. Look at Lola and Taju just back from America.

BABA: Eh – so! *(Nonsense.)* Weren't they deported?

SIS RONKE: Baba! You were there when they burned their green cards! They chose to come back, and from Atlanta, one of the best cities for black people in US. University of Ibadan and Harvard grads. They can go anywhere. They chose Nigeria.

BABA: Someone must have put something in their food!

SIS RONKE: Baba! Why shouldn't they come back? We used to have 'brain drain.' Now we have 'brain gain', for the new Nigeria.

BABA: New Nigeria? Re-branding nonsense! How can you re-brand, when there has never even been a brand?

SIS RONKE: We're rebuilding, Baba, not just re-branding.

BABA: It's a lie! Nigeria is as rotten as ever!

SIS RONKE: Baba! You are not patriotic. After what Fashola has achieved in Lagos? In public order, in sanitation, in transport? And the other governors are already following suit. Even the Sultan of Sokoto sent his own governor to consult with him.

BABA: Toyin, millions unemployed. Graduates wandering the streets. Students rioting. Social protests. Turmoil.

MAMA-RONKE: As in London! And he claims he reads the papers! Didn't you read about our riots?

BABA: Armed robbers on the loose. Security is nowhere – instead police who should protect us are extorting money from motorists with impunity. Where is the rule of law? Ransom kidnapping so rife in some areas people are afraid to venture out. Our cities collapsing – look around you - creaking with ramshackle infrastructure – decrepit roads, decrepit buildings. And rural areas are even worse, like … back in the stone-age. People are starving! I've said it before and I'll say it again: Nigeria is a tinderbox waiting to explode.

MAMA-RONKE: People have been suffering for decades. And then what?

BABA: And then a man set himself alight in Tunisia and a fire has started. Hey! It will soon spread down the Nile. It's coming throughout Africa, so we better get ready. Toyin, I want to tell you some bitter truth. I want to knock some truth right into your head. We are comfortable, but the masses – kai! – they've had enough. Fela said it, he warned us, and now the original sufferheads are ready to fight for a better life. I saw Taofiki and the gateman talking outside o. *(To RONKE.)* The people you bully and harass because they are poor. They are getting ready! Mobilising! Fela said it. Water, light, food, house – Ye paripa o!

MAMA-RONKE smiles, recognizing the opening lines from one of Fela's hits.

BABA: That mean to say you no dey for Nigeria be that. You see yourself, you no dey for Africa at all. You must dey come from London, from New York, Brazil, Germany, Frankfurt, Rome, Italy, Spanish, Portugal, Arabia, from Moscow, Chicago. That mean to say you no dey for Nigeria be that. If you dey for Africa where we dey, you go know …

MAMA-RONKE: I go know wetin?

BABA: You go know! They wey dey for London them dey live like lords. Those wey dey for New York them dey live like kings. We wey dey for Africa we dey live like servants …

MAMA-RONKE: Ok, ok. It's enough.

BABA: *(Pursuing her.)* Them come turn us to suffer head o!

MAMA-RONKE: Thank you, Fela number 2.

BABA: *(Scolding RONKE.)* I say sufferhead must go! Treat your workers properly o!

SIS RONKE: That Fela was a rascal. Don't mind him.

BABA: *(To TOYIN.)* And don't leave your son here to suffer o!

MAMA-RONKE: *(Interrupting.)* OK, OK, brother, let's eat. I know you're hungry. The rice and stew are ready…

BABA: I don't want to eat. So you can ply me with palm wine like yesterday? To make me nod off again?

MAMA-RONKE: No, no, no, no. And, besides, I need your help to find something. The keys for my boxes.

BABA: Joh! I know your tricks. Toyin, listen carefully…

TOYIN: I'm listening. I'm listening.

SIS RONKE: Eat, Baba. We will listen. You'll speak better when you've eaten.

BABA: *(To MAMA.)* What kind of stew?

MAMA-RONKE: Okra. Buky will prepare semolina with it, or pounded yam? And there's some palm wine left.

BABA: Buky leaves too many lumps. Ask Bisi instead.
Toyin, pack Rotimi's things now! And don't sign anything.
Sho'g bo me? Mon'bo *[I'm coming back].*

MAMA bundles him out as SIS RONKE goes to the window and leans out.

SIS RONKE: *(Bellowing out.)* Taofiki. Ki lon se ni bi gate yen?
Why are you loitering at the gate? Stop gossiping with
Sunday and go and continue your duties. If I see you there
again, I will injure you! And remove that bucket from my car.

TOYIN sinks into the sofa, nodding vigorously to herself.

SIS RONKE: *(Sitting.)* Idiots! Enemies of progress.

TOYIN: He's right. He's right!

SIS RONKE: Who? Baba? Look, Nigeria has problems, yes.
Doesn't the UK? They're even doing austerity measures,
and all such things, just as we had here in the eighties and
nineties. See IMF and World Bank at work in Greece and
Spain! My friend, the world is changing. Angola is giving
aid and loans to Portugal, its former colonial master. Can
you imagine! India and China - weren't they so-called
'Third World' a decade ago? Look at them now. Let me tell
you, seven out of the ten fastest growing economies in the
world are in Africa. Yes! Kenya, Tanzania and Uganda are
growing like China and India. Oh yes! They used to talk
about Asian tigers. Well, we are the African lions! The wheel
is still turning. Write it on the wall: Africa is rising.

TOYIN shakes her head stubbornly, rising.

TOYIN: Give me a break. Please!

SIS RONKE: Come back in fifty years, my friend. You'll see.

*TOYIN exits. BEV enters, looking a little disheveled, but triumphantly
counting some naira.*

SIS RONKE: Ah ah. No, no, no, no. It's impossible!

BEV: 3,700, 3,800, 3,900…

SIS RONKE: You mean they gave it back! Impossible.

BEV: *(Folding it away.)* I don't like being ripped off.

SIS RONKE: Ah ha. This is news! No Nigerian has ever been
known to give a refund. Anyway, it's because they're from
Togo. That's why.

BEV: I'm going to give it back to them tomorrow. It's just the
principle.

SIS RONKE: Yes. You're right. Principle. And probity. That's what must be the foundation of the new Nigeria.

BEV sits next to SIS RONKE and opens the mag. To business.

BEV: Sis Ronke, I loved what you said in here about expanding telecoms in Africa.

SIS RONKE takes it.

SIS RONKE: Oh, this is out already.

She flicks through. Nods satisfied, even smug.

BEV: Did you get a chance to look at my CV?

SIS RONKE: Ah yes. I did. In fact, why are you wasting your time in that job in London? You're overqualified for it, abi?

BEV: Yes! Big time. But lots of us can't find any work at all. Forget qualifications. Your face has to fit.

SIS RONKE: It's their loss. Anyway, your ideas were very…

BEV: Wait, I've developed them even more! I reread the sector report. There's millions of people with phones but no way to get formal financial services. So why not serve them with mobile wallets? We can expand banking services all over West Africa…

SIS RONKE: OK.

BEV: …sim card opportunities, number portability… I reckon vehicle tracking systems will be big in telecoms soon too…

SIS RONKE: I'm saying yes.

BEV: What?

SIS RONKE: Yes. Develop the business plan. You can help me with the convention too. But you'll be in Shanghai for a month.

BEV: Thank you! Thank you so much, Sis Ronke. I'll work so hard, I won't let you down…

SIS: I know. I saw your CV!

BEV: But you're paying me in dollars or sterling, right?

SIS RONKE: What's wrong with naira?

BEV: I've gotta pay my mortgage in London. Until I find tenants.

SIS RONKE: Oh, so our currency isn't good enough for you, eh?

BEV: Actually, make it sterling.

SIS RONKE: Euros.

BEV: No way!

SIS RONKE: We'll decide later. What about this your Dipo?

BEV: Dapo.

SIS RONKE: Dipo. Dapo. E wo lo on ninu omo elede *[what's the difference]?* Whatever you call him. You are still associating with him?

BEV: You're all worrying too much. He's a decent, honest guy. He's got a good business. Import-export.

SIS RONKE: Hey! Wahala for you! Look o, Bev! This man. This Dayo…

BEV: Dapo. Dapo. DAPO…

MAMA-RONKE enters, holding another bunch of keys.

MAMA-RONKE: *(Correcting her.)* Dapo. At least pronounce it the right way. So, you're still mixing with that riff-raff?

BEV: Look, he's a decent, honest guy…

MAMA-RONKE: Wahala for you! Look o! I am an African. I was born and raised here. I spent twenty-eight years in Nigeria before I went to Europe. I know my people. You don't understand the language. You don't know the culture. You don't know about this our rituals. I'm warning you. Don't play with fire.

BEV: Aunty Pandora, you can meet him. I'll bring him here.

TIMI enters as SIS RONKE snorts in amusement.

SIS RONKE: As if he'd dare face us. He knows we'll see right through him. 419er! Crook!

MAMA-RONKE: Why didn't he come to the send-off party?

BEV: He had some business to deal with.

SIS RONKE: Fraudster! Invite him again. See if he dares come.

BEV: He'll come. He even took me to his mum's.

SIS RONKE: His mum?

BEV: Yes, I went to her house.

SIS RONKE: Her house! Or so you think. He probably just hired one useless Nollywood actress.

MAMA-RONKE: And gave her 20,000 naira to pose as his mother. *(Picking up a DVD from the table.)* Is this her? *(Thrusting it under BEV's nose.)* Look! Isn't this your so-called mother-in-law?

They laugh, but BEV ignores them and calmly takes the DVD. But as she's about to toss it aside, she takes a closer look, peering at the face, a bit worried.

SIS RONKE: *(To MAMA.)* Next, he'll be telling her his mother is sick and needs money for an operation.

MAMA-RONKE: Or that his home is about to be repossessed. Romance fraud! Ole! *(To BEV.)* He'll ask you to take out loans or overdrafts. He might even lure you somewhere, kidnap you and then demand a ransom.

BEV puts the DVD down slowly, thoughtfully.

BEV: OK, I'll bring him. I'll go tell him now. He's only round the corner.

MAMA-RONKE: Do your worst. I won't let you kill me. And this foolish trunk… I'm getting fed up with this…

TIMI: *(To BEV.)* I'm coming. I want another ride in his Benz.

TOYIN re-enters.

BEV: Come on, then. Oh, Toyin, just taking Timi out for a spin. You OK?

TOYIN nods, though she's clearly not.

MAMA-RONKE: I can't believe it. This is ridiculous!

She flings the whole bunch down.

TIMI: Granny, I can open it.

TOYIN: Mum, calm down. Timi, don't break it.

MAMA-RONKE: We've only got a few hours left…

But TIMI's got a little wire thing he's using and…hey presto. The lock springs opens. MAMA claps her hands.

MAMA-RONKE: At last! How did you do it?

TIMI: Man's got skills.

BEV: Skills? How did you learn those 'skills?'

TIMI: That's for me to know. Man's gotta do what a man's gotta do, get me?

TIMI and BEV exit, she twisting his ear as they go.

BEV: Oh, so you're a 'man' now?

TOYIN: *(Excited.)* Gosh. I don't believe it's actually opened.

SIS RONKE: What's the big deal? It's just a trunk. Everyone who comes back from London has one?

TOYIN and SIS RONKE crowd round as MAMA-RONKE dips in.

TOYIN: But I've never seen what's inside. It was like forbidden fruit. 'Never go near my trunk. Don't let me see you tampering with my trunk…' Blimey. I thought there were dead bodies in it.

MAMA fishes around and pulls out a dress. She unfolds it and holds it up.

SIS RONKE: I hope that's not for me.

MAMA-RONKE: What do you mean? It's a very popular style.

TOYIN: It was. A long time ago.

RONKE: Ma'mi, we don't wear that sort of thing anymore.

MAMA-RONKE: *(Indignant.)* Oh, so this is not good enough for you? I bought this in C&A of Oxford Street.

TOYIN: C&A closed down years ago, mum. It's a Primark now.

MAMA-RONKE: Na you sabi. It's your loss. *(Folding it.)* I'll send it to my people in Ibadan. They'll appreciate it.

RONKE fishes around inside the trunk. She takes out a doll. She jumps as TOYIN screams.

TOYIN: That's mine!

SIS RONKE: What?

TOYIN: *(Pouncing and grabbing.)* It's her. It's mine. She's mine. That's the doll I asked for when I was 8.

MAMA-RONKE: I bought it for you.

TOYIN: Then you said you hadn't bought it, but I knew. I knew I'd seen it in a bag and I thought you'd given it to someone else.

MAMA-RONKE: I bought it for you.

TOYIN: So why didn't you give it to me, Mum?

MAMA-RONKE looks tearful. She shakes her head. RONKE dips in again and takes out a dress. It's ghastly – lemon yellow taffeta with a petticoat.

TOYIN: And that dress…that's the…yes…that's the dress from Marks and Spencer. I begged you for it on my 10th birthday.

MAMA-RONKE is nodding again.

SIS RONKE: It's ugly, anyway.

TOYIN: No it's not. Everyone else in my class had one, except me. All the things I wanted. You bought them, and then locked them away! Why?

MAMA-RONKE: I don't know.

TOYIN: It doesn't make sense.

MAMA-RONKE: I know, but I didn't know what else to do. I wanted to be fair…to the two of you…but you were on two different continents.

TOYIN and RONKE look at each other.

TOYIN: Look at all the things I missed out on.

SIS RONKE: I'm the one who missed out.

TOYIN: Oh, please!

MAMA-RONKE: I don't know why… I thought I was being fair… Instead, maybe I failed both of you.

SIS RONKE: Yes, you did.

MAMA is stung and goes to leave.

TOYIN: No, she didn't. Mum, you didn't. Don't listen to her. *(To RONKE.)* What's wrong with you?

TOYIN tries to follows MAMA. RONKE stops her, on the warpath. Time to have it out.

SIS RONKE: She wanted to talk, didn't she? So let's talk.

SIS RONKE moves to leave, but TOYIN restrains her.

TOYIN: Give her a break.

SIS RONKE: She's finally realising the damage she did. Good.

She tries to pull away, TOYIN holds tight.

TOYIN: She's been trying to talk to you since we got here. Now a few hours before we leave…

SIS RONKE: *(Pulling away.)* Oto oro o kan. *[Home truths are bitter].* Some home truths are way overdue.

TOYIN: She did her best.

SIS RONKE: Ra, ra o! *[I disagree]* It wasn't good enough.

MAMA-RONKE re-enters, RONKE wheels round.

MAMA-RONKE: From Taofiki to your sister. From your sister to me. Whoever you can vent your frustrations on. Well, I'm not your houseboy, nor am I your junior sister. You're quick to condemn Timi for lack of respect to his elders. What of you? Is this respect? I'm your...

SIS RONKE: Iya mi. My mother, abi?

MAMA-RONKE: *(Deep breath.)* You can refuse me as your mother, but don't forget this – I'm not your age mate. I won't tolerate your rudeness anymore! Don't let me say something I'll regret. I'm warning you. If I open my mouth, it will stick.

SIS RONKE: Do your worst. E se epe funmi te ba se! E so nkon ta ba fe so! *[Curse me if you like! Say what you want. Am I bothered?]*

MAMA-RONKE: *(Superhuman control.)* Ronke, let me pack my loads and go. I'm sorry I bothered you by coming here. I won't do so again. It's nearly nine. In no time I'll be leaving your house.

SIS RONKE: Yes, you're leaving. Leaving again. Well, the first time you left I was too young to speak up. But I can speak now.

MAMA-RONKE: And you've spoken. Very clearly. I failed. That's what you said. I'm a bad mother.

SIS RONKE: I've got some other things to say...

MAMA-RONKE: I don't have to explain myself to you or to anyone else. I am your mother. I did what I thought was best.

SIS RONKE: For you!

MAMA-RONKE: No, for you!

SIS RONKE: E duro na! *[Hold up! Wait a minute!]* That was best...leaving me behind? E fi mi fe le! *[You left me!]*

MAMA-RONKE: Yes, I left you behind. At the time, that's what I thought was best...

SIS RONKE: I want you to apologise.

MAMA-RONKE: For what?

TOYIN: Leave her alone, Ronke. She did her best.

SIS RONKE: I want you to admit that you abandoned me. I want you to say you're sorry...

TOYIN: Leave my mum alone!

MAMA-RONKE: I've said it, haven't I?

SIS RONKE: No, you always say, 'maybe I made a mistake' or 'perhaps I was wrong.' But it's not maybe, it's not perhaps. Both you and my dad left me and didn't come back.

MAMA-RONKE: We went to study. We didn't mean to stay.

SIS RONKE: Say sorry.

MAMA-RONKE: What was I supposed to do? I couldn't come, once I had Toyin and the others in London.

SIS RONKE: Say you're sorry.

TOYIN: Leave her alone. Mum, let's just go.

MAMA-RONKE: I couldn't be in two places at once. And I thought you were better off here.

SIS RONKE: SAY IT.

MAMA looks from one to the other, trying to find the answer. She sinks down.

MAMA-RONKE: I didn't succeed at all. I didn't even finish my studies. What I went there for, I didn't even achieve. And you paid the price. You're right. I'm sorry. Yes, I'm sorry.

SIS RONKE turns away. The apology she wanted isn't soothing.

MAMA-RONKE: *(Picking up the dress.)* Buying things and storing them up for years. I don't know why. Because I was too proud to come home without my qualifications. I did it all wrong.

SIS RONKE: I don't want your dolls, or dresses, or…

She starts tossing the dresses, dolls and other gifts back at the trunk, but they're flying everywhere but into it. Finished, she slumps onto the sofa, a spent force.

SIS RONKE: Take them back. I don't want them… I want…

She trails off. MAMA rises with whatever strength she can muster and stumbles out. TOYIN looks at RONKE, furiously.

TOYIN: You got your pound of flesh. Happy now?

SIS RONKE: I remember the day I met our dad. The one and only time. I was in form five. He came to my boarding house. I was called out of biology – it was near the end of the lesson – and when I got to the Principal's office, she said 'there's someone special here to see you, a visitor from

England.' And there he was, a tall, slim man, standing by her desk, looking out of the window, in a grey suit and a red bow tie. I knew who he was straight away. He stayed for about an hour, we walked around the garden together, then he gave me some money and he left. And I never saw him again. He sent presents through his mother. For a few years. *(Pauses.)* A visitor from England.

TOYIN: In London, he lived about twenty minutes away, but we never saw him.

SIS RONKE: Neither of them came back for me.

TOYIN: But you had Africa, the motherland.

SIS RONKE: *(Crumbling.)* But you had a mother.

She gets up and exits as BEV and TIMI arrive back.

TIMI: He wasn't in. His car wasn't there either…

BEV: Hey, what happened here? Oh, I recognise that dress …!

TOYIN just grabs TIMI and clasps him to her.

End of scene two.

SCENE THREE

9pm. The front room is empty apart from TIMI on the Playstation. Just then, the doorbell rings.

SIS RONKE: *(Shouting off stage.)* Taofiki? Can't you hear? See who it is. *(Pause.)* Please.

Seconds later a teenage BOY enters. This is TIMI's cousin, TOPE (15). He's wearing an agbada and carrying a Bible. He sneaks up behind TIMI and whips off the hat. TIMI turns, sees him and leaps up...and they both go nuts. They can't be cool – it's been too long.

TIMI: Oh my dayz. Tops! The man himself!

TOPE: Timi!

They leap around, hugging and laughing.

TOPE: London boy! You did it. You came to Naija. I can't believe it.

TIMI: Going back tonight, cuz! *(Rapping from B.I.G.)* 'Isn't it great, my flight leaves at eight...'

TOPE: *(Joining in.)* 'Your flight leaves at nine, My game's just rewind...'

They're rocking and rapping as one in an instant.

TIMI/TOPE: 'lyrically I'm supposed to represent; I'm not only the client, I am the player president.'

SIS RONKE re-enters. Her face is a bit puffy, eyes a bit red, but she'll always keep going. She knows her duty. She looks on aghast as they romp around.

SIS RONKE: You two. Stop this rubbish and nonsense.

TOPE: *(Leaping over and prostrating.)* Hello, Auntie Ronke.

TIMI looks at him in amazement.

TIMI: BRUV!!!

SIS RONKE: Welcome, Tope. How are you, my dear?

TOPE: *(Switching code to Naija mode.)* Fine, thank you, Auntie. God is looking after us well. Auntie, are you OK?

SIS RONKE: I'm fine. I'm fine. Sho ti jeun?

TOPE: Pardon, Auntie?

SIS RONKE: Tope, ah ah. Still no Yoruba after one year! I said, sho ti jeun? Have you eaten?

TOPE: Oh, yes, thank you, Auntie.

SIS RONKE: A Yoruba boy who does not speak Yoruba! It's a pity. Anyway, where is Principal Osun?

As she speaks, the bell goes again.

SIS RONKE: That must be him.

As she exits they collapse back onto the sofa.

SIS RONKE: *(Offstage.)* Taofiki! You fool! Do I have to call you each time?

TIMI: *(Looking him over.)* Tops! 'Member when we used to go ice-skating every Friday?

TOPE: And Karate, swimming class, go-carting down the sports centre. Football after school.

TIMI: The good old days.

TOPE: With Akin, Kayode, Drew, Nick...all the mandem!

TIMI: Innit! All my soldiers!

TOPE: How are they? How are you all doing? How you dey now?

TIMI: Safe, man. Everyone's fine. What's 'gwaning with you?

TOPE: I dey, o! Where'd you get those trainers?

TIMI: Niketown, son.

TOPE: Niketown! Trocadero! West End! I remember, I remember!

TIMI: But, bruv, what are YOU wearing?

TOPE: Shut up! It's what we all wear. I'm an African man.

TIMI: Joker! I still can't believe it. About Tops. In Nigeria! In boarding school!

TOPE: Yuh get me doh! *(Waving his Bible.)* G to G!

TIMI: Say what?

TOPE: Sorry. I keep saying it. Means Glory to God. From Bible Class.

TIMI: Yeah, well. Calm down. Tops-man, got bare things to tell you. But you can't tell anyone...

TOPE: What is it? Tell me, tell me...

TIMI: Can you keep a secret? This is proper classified.

TOPE: 'Course!

TIMI: Nah, nah, it's OK.

TOPE: Tell me!

TIMI: OK, guess what I'm joining when I get back?

He's interrupted as MAMA-RONKE enters. Another sombre, puffy face. She's drained, but she's bearing up. She carries a light coat. Both boys straighten up pronto, like in Toy Story when the humans enter.

MAMA-RONKE: Tope, my dear! I heard you'd arrived.

TOPE: Ssshhh. Tell me later. *(Prostrating again.)* Good evening, Ma.

TIMI gives him the same look of amazement.

MAMA-RONKE: *(Hugging him.)* Welcome, Tope. How are you?

TOPE: *(Switching code to Naija again.)* Fine, thank you, Ma.

MAMA-RONKE: Hey, proper Naija man! How are you enjoying Nigeria?

TOPE: It's fine, Ma. But are you OK? You look sad.

MAMA-RONKE: I'm fine. I'm fine. Have you eaten?

TOPE: Yes, ma. Thank you, ma.

MAMA-RONKE: Good.

She picks up a suitcase to move it. TOPE swoops over and carries it for her. She smiles and pats him on the back.

MAMA-RONKE: Well done. You're a good example.

TOPE smirks at TIMI who is staring at him in amazement.

TIMI: Tops, are you on crack!

BABA enters. TOPE moves to prostrate again but BABA yanks him back upright.

BABA: Joh, get up, stand up. All this bowing and scraping. It's unnecessary. See that, Pandora? Why should our children bow, like, like minions? How can they become confident when they are so downtrodden? That's why they grow up to let rogues and vagabonds seize power and bully them. They learn deference in childhood.

MAMA-RONKE: Oh, you want to see confidence? Come and see them in London! They're running wild! We say we mustn't abuse them, then they start abusing us.

BABA: So our children should fear us? Is that good?

MAMA-RONKE: Joh, it's not my own. Talk to the mother. I'm tired of this whole matter!

BABA: What of the emotional effects? Those children dragged here, how many of them are really happy?

MAMA-RONKE: Sshhh. They'll hear. Look at Tope. He is. Look.

BABA: You should have seen him last year. It could have ended differently o. What of Mrs Onitola's son? The one they sent from Manchester. Fine, handsome boy. What was his name? I've forgotten. That one nearly starved himself to death. They rushed him back to England a wreck. Will he ever recover?

MAMA-RONKE: Anyway, I did my best.

BABA: Eh-hen. Deji! Ada fun e. That was his name. Deji. Poor boy.

MAMA-RONKE: What about Jide? Mrs Akinwande's last born? After two years HE loved it so much he refused to go back to London. His brothers and sisters begged their mother to send them. Look, she must decide for herself. Every mother does her best. I did my best. I did.

BABA: Oh, don't worry about Ronke. That is how she was, even as a child. Always so dramatic. She'll soon calm down.

MAMA exits. BABA following as he speaks, but loud beeping from outside makes him pause to peek out of the window.

BABA: Yey! How can he park there! *(Shouting.)* Hey! You this man, remove your vehicle. You're blocking my own. Hey! You de craze!

He runs out to deal with the situation. TIMI is still staring at TOPE, shaking his head.

TIMI: Tops, you've changed.

TOPE: No, I haven't.

TIMI: You won't catch me kneeling down.

TOPE: Allow it. That's what I said at first. We all do it. When I met the Oba…

TIMI: Who?

TOPE: The king, of course. When I went to his palace I had to proper roll on the ground in front of him. We all did.

TIMI: That's peer pressure, blud! Just say no, cuz.

TOPE cracks up.

TIMI: What?

59

TOPE: Cuz. Blud.

TIMI: What? What you laughing at?

TOPE: Ha ha ha. Oh man! You're just reminding me.

TIMI: What's so funny?

TOPE: I used to say all that stuff, didn't I?

TIMI: Say all what?

TOPE: Bruv, cuz, all that. I forgot. I used to say that too.

TIMI: So?

TOPE: *(Wiping his eyes.)* Nothing, nothing. The good old days. I just forgot all that stuff. Anyway, where is it?

TIMI: *(Smiling.)* Bruv, you're not ready.

TOPE: Shut up, you fool and let me see.

> *TIMI produces his phone and dangles it in TOPE's face.*

TIMI: Latest iPhone, bredren. The latest model. I've apps for everything. Everything. Let me show you my Instagram.

> *They huddle over the phone, ignoring SIS RONKE entering with a MAN.*

> *This is PRINCIPAL OSUN (50), an energetic, quick-eyed man. He's a graduate of the University of Lagos, (BA Philosophy); LSE, London (MA Educational Development); and HARVARD, USA (MBA). He has an evangelical zeal about him. He's not only intelligent, he IS intelligence.*

SIS RONKE: You're welcome, sir. Please, Sis E joko *[do sit down]*. My sister is coming.

PRIN OSUN: *(Sitting.)* Ronke, you are looking fine. Se alaafia ni? *[How is everyone/everything?]*

SIS RONKE: A dupe *[We thank God]*. We are managing. What can I offer you?

PRIN OSUN: I'll just take a soft drink.

SIS RONKE: *(Calling.)* TAOFIKI.

PRIN OSUN: Thank you for your generous donation.

SIS RONKE: Don't mention it.

PRIN OSUN: And have you decided about standing for the state election?

SIS RONKE: You know I'm just a businesswoman. I told you and the committee that last time. I'm not a politician.

PRIN OSUN: Come on, you business people are our government. You know that.

SIS RONKE: OK, OK, we'll discuss.

PRIN OSUN: Good. *(Looking at TIMI.)* Is that the boy?

SIS RONKE: Hmmnn. Yes, that's my nephew. Rotimi, come.

TIMI gets up and comes over. PRIN OSUN waits. TIMI just stands there, erect.

TIMI: Hello.

SIS RONKE: *(To TIMI.)* Prostrate, now!

PRIN OSUN: Don't worry. They are all like that at first. We soon knock them into shape. Hello, young man.

TIMI: Hello.

SIS RONKE is about to reprimand him but the PRINCIPAL raises a hand for her not to speak. She stops. TIMI looks like he wants to go back and sit down but he doesn't move. It's like he's transfixed. The PRINCIPAL is holding his gaze. He rises and faces TIMI, towering over him. He holds out his hand. TIMI takes it.

PRIN OSUN: How are you?

His voice, that of an adult male in his prime, sounds strange after all the female voices we've been hearing so far. TIMI cocks his head at the strange sound.

TIMI: Fine. *(He inexplicably finds himself adding.)* Sir.

Just then TOYIN enters. She looks apprehensive.

SIS RONKE: Toyin, this is Principal Osun. Principal, my aburo from London, Toyin.

TOYIN: How do you do? Welcome.

PRIN OSUN releases TIMI's hand, but still holds his gaze. He holds out his hand to TOYIN who shakes it. She curtsies, awkwardly. TIMI just looks at her.

TIMI: What's got into everyone?

TOYIN looks at him.

TOYIN: Timi, are you OK?

TIMI: Uh huh.

TOYIN looks from him to the PRINCIPAL, not sure what's going on. She puts her arms around TIMI protectively.

PRIN OSUN: *(Indicating TIMI.)* So, madam, I've come to pick your fruit.

TIMI looks at his mum quizzically. TOYIN twitches.

TOYIN: Yes, well, I…

Just then TOPE bounds over and touches her on the back. She turns and jumps with joy.

TOYIN: Topsy! My baby! How are you?

They hug.

TOPE: Hello, Aunty Toyin.

TOYIN: Look how big you are! And your skin! Look at it, it's so beautiful.

PRIN OSUN: African sunshine. I keep telling you people you should come home. Our fruit blossoms here. Well done for bringing the young man…

TOYIN: *(Hurriedly.)* Yes. Err, yes. OK, Timi, Tope, why don't you guys go out and buy some drinks. Here, take this. *(She thrusts some money at them.)* But don't go far; we're leaving soon.

TIMI: Come on, man.

TOPE: OK, But I wanna change. Let me wear some of your garms.

TIMI: OK. I got a new top upstairs. But you can't keep it.

TOPE: Sweet, Cuz. Blud. Bruv. Ha ha ha.

They troop out. The adults sit down.

TOYIN: Sorry to interrupt like that. I…he…

PRIN OSUN: Not at all. Not at all. I understand. We've had cases of youths running away. It's best to leave telling them to the last possible minute.

TOYIN: Well, the thing is…

PRIN OSUN: And I can see why you need him with us.

He and SIS RONKE exchange a knowing glance which TOYIN intercepts and does not like at all.

TOYIN: *(Defensive.)* Oh?

PRIN OSUN: My dear, you've made the right choice. And not a moment too soon.

He gestures for her to sit down.

TOYIN: Thank you so very much, but it just so happens…

PRIN OSUN: I congratulate you on acting so swiftly. I look into his eyes and it's clear…

TOYIN: What is clear?

PRIN OSUN: I can see how far down the road he's gone.

TOYIN: The road. Which road?

PRIN OSUN: That's why they call me the gangster catcher. From London, from Los Angeles, from all over the diaspora, they bring them to me. I take those unruly boys and turn them into men. And I find the worst trouble-makers often turn out to make the best leaders.

TOYIN: Excuse me, my son isn't a trouble-maker…

PRIN OSUN: Indeed, he has great potential. I read the application, and I could see what's in him when I met him just now. He wants to be in charge. That's good. Those are the ones we pick. He's coming to one of the top schools in Africa because of that potential. A place at Wide Horizons Academy does not come easily. You know you missed the deadline by seven months. I turned down the son of the Vice-Chancellor of Lagos University, as a special favour to your sister.

SIS RONKE: Tell her.

He opens his briefcase and produces a lavish brochure.

PRIN OSUN: I think you've seen pictures of our campus.

TOYIN nods.

PRIN OSUN: Here is the new science lab. Here is the new theatre. As an institution we believe in mixing excellence with innovation, discipline with creativity. That's why we attract the best. We are the best. From tomorrow your son will be mixing with the cream of Africa. At Wide Horizons Academy we have the sons of kings and queens, ambassadors, politicians, professors. He'll be mixing with the leaders of tomorrow's world.

SIS RONKE: If she only knew. It's one of the best schools in Africa.

PRIN OSUN: Ah, madam, don't be confused, o! Wide Horizons is more than a good school! It is much, much more. It is in fact a…a transformation chamber.

SIS RONKE: Amen.

PRIN OSUN: You see that Tope? Wasn't he a member of some wild group of ruffians in London?

SIS RONKE: He was a gang member.

TOYIN: The Get Rich Quick crew was not exactly a gang…

PRIN OSUN: Whatever. Tope is now a member of the VIPs. That's the clique he hangs out with at school. They do stocks and shares on the internet. On the internet! One of their fathers runs Veritas Bank of Africa. They are the leaders of tomorrow. Is that not the kind of man you want YOUR son to be?

TOYIN: I think I should tell you…

PRIN OSUN: No, of course. You don't have to answer. It's as clear to you as it is to me. Let me guess. So a few months ago…maybe even a year…you looked into his eyes and saw something new. A look you didn't recognize, or like.

TOYIN: No. Well, sort of…yes, he was different but…

PRIN OSUN: He was changing, am I right?

TOYIN: No…well, yes. But he's a teenager. They all go through phases. And a friend of his was…He's not a bad boy… Where's Baba?

SIS RONKE: Moving his car. Focus.

PRIN OSUN: *(To RONKE.)* Changing. *(He turns back to TOYIN.)* It's always the same. First, he's bright eyed and bushy tailed. Doing his homework on time, enjoying getting good marks, leaping up to let old ladies sit down on the bus. Praised by everyone. The apple of your eye. Then, somehow, somehow, he loses interest in school. He's there, oh yes, but now he sits in class staring out of the window. What is he thinking about? He tells you school is boring. He doesn't like the work. His results start to slip and he begins to play up in class. Worse, he's beginning to get home late from school; then later and later. When he is back, he's off out again and disappears till midnight, *(Off her expression.)* or later. And now all sorts of people are calling for him at home, at all hours, people of a different sort to the friends he used to mix with. They call him by a strange name and he says it's just his nickname. The school reports worsen, there are minor incidents, but it's always 'all a terrible mistake, mum'…

TOYIN gasps.

PRIN OSUN: ...and you believe him. You want to believe him. You have to believe him because you're helpless. There's no role model to help him change into the kind of man you wanted him to be. You talk to him, you plead with him, you bribe him: iPods, iPads, the latest phones, clothes, hey! But to no avail...he's still changing, now so fast, sometimes you don't recognize the cheerful boy he was just two years ago. Those moods, so strange. So gradually you accept the truth: you need help. You have to let him go. And now the time has come.

TOYIN has sat through this like he's reading from the book of her life. PRIN OSUN reaches into his briefcase again and pulls a piece of paper out. He stands and places it on the trunk.

PRIN OSUN: So, here's the contract. You're signing to save him. Are you ready?

TOYIN: Well... I... I...

PRIN OSUN: His future starts here.

PRIN OSUN pushes the paper towards her and hands her his pen.

She looks at it, hesitates, then looks at him, shaking her head, but reaches for the pen at the same time. She had made up her mind, but the dithering, the doubt...here they come, rising up again. She takes the pen. She moves to sign, then stops, she moves again, but can't.

TOYIN: I'm sorry... I mean...can you wait... I just need a moment...please.

End of scene three.

SCENE FOUR

We're outside MAMA AMAKA's 'TEKAWAY' chop shop.

TOPE and TIMI are sitting on a bench taking photos with the phone. Lagos traffic blares past. Fuji music is playing somewhere in the background. Snatches of conversation in Yoruba waft by.

TOPE has a hoodie on over his agbada and is trying on one of TIMI's trainers.

TIMI: I think it's disgraceful.

TOPE: Twice on Sundays, and twice during the week.

TIMI: Why d'you go church so much?

TOPE: Everybody does. These trainers look better on me.

TIMI: They're brand new.

TOPE: Just for an hour.

TIMI: *(Taking the other one off.)* OK.

TOPE: Where d'you get them again?

TIMI: Nike Town.

TOPE: Where'd you get the money?

TIMI: My mum, of course. I got the red ones too.

TOPE: My mum said your mum was gonna send you to my school.

TIMI: No way. She did ask me, but I squashed it. I ain't coming to no dry-up place. Call me nuts, but when I turn on a tap, I wannna see water flow. When I flip a switch I'm looking light! Get me?

TOPE: Yeah, but you just use a generator. At school we get electricity all the time. These creps are craaazeeee! Man, wish my mum was like yours.

TIMI: My mum is soft. Your mum is hardcore. A female Mr T.

TOPE: *(Singing the ditty from 'Fresh Prince'.)* I got in one little fight and my mum got scared…

TIMI/TOPE: 'She said you're moving in with your aunt and uncle in… Nigeria!!!'

TOPE: I wouldn't mind if it was Bel Air!

TIMI: Fuh real! Now that's what I'm talking 'bout.

TOPE looks away and is quiet for a while.

TOPE: I miss her though.

TIMI: 'Course. She's still your mum.

TOPE: When she left me here, I didn't talk to her for three months.

TIMI: She wasn't hardcore when she left you here, though. She was crying at our house for days.

TOPE: *(Amazed.)* Crying.

TIMI: For weeks!

TOPE: Why?

TIMI: Cos she missed you, of course!

TOPE absorbs this.

TOPE: Missed me?

TIMI looks at him, nodding.

TOPE: What, was she really, REALLY crying?

TIMI: YEEES. All over my settee, bruv.

TOPE: I thought she didn't...want me anymore.

TIMI: You just disappeared, man. We didn't know what had happened to you. Then some new boy took your desk. Some Kosovan. Stefan wouldn't let him sit down for weeks.

TIMI catches TOPE's downcast expression.

TIMI: Anyway, it's all good. You're coming home soon. You can keep that top, you know.

TOPE: *(Still miserable.)* Really? Thanks.

TIMI: Nigeria's alright, Tops. They do some funny shit, don't they? When we went to the village to visit our relatives, they killed a chicken right in front of us. I half-fainted.

TOPE: Oh, I've seen that loads of times. One day I was playing with this really cute goat. The next day, I asked them where it was, and they pointed to my plate!

TIMI: But what about them pictures in our great-great-grandfather's house?

TOPE: Yeah man! I couldn't believe it!

TIMI: Me as a baby, you as a baby, my birthday parties, all my school pictures. My mum and your mum when they were kids. They even had pictures of me I hadn't seen myself!

TOPE: Were they chanting all them prayers, and telling you all that history stuff? You know, like how that village is named after our great-grandfather? It's true, you know? We studied it in Yoruba history – how our ancestors migrated from the north to the south and settled in Oyo…

TIMI: Yeah, yeah, they were chatting all that olden day stuff. What you looking forward to most when you come back to London?

TOPE: McDonalds! Only two in Lagos. But we got Tantalizers. That's good. And Mr Bigs.

TIMI: What? Do they do sizzlers?

TOPE: No, they do jollof and pepper chicken and things like that. It's good.

TOPE starts to sing a fast-food chain jingle in Yoruba.

TOPE: 'Ki lo fee je? Se o fee j'eba? Rara, mi o fee j'eba. Sizzlers ni mo fee je!' *[What do you want to eat? Eba? No. I don't want to eat eba. I want to eat Sizzlers.]*

TIMI: But…hold up…I thought you didn't understand Yoruba?

TOPE: And don't you go blabbing! I don't want them to know.

TIMI: Why not?

TOPE: They'll expect me to…do more. And they won't say as much in front of me. I know everything that's going on, cos they don't bother what they say when I'm around. Shall I teach you some?

TIMI: Shuuuut up. Hey, Tope, remember that girl you liked?

TOPE: Which girl?

TIMI: That one from the flats near my house. Jennifer.

TOPE: Tall, slim ting?

TIMI: Yeah.

TOPE: Jennifer. Yeah, yeah, yeah.

TIMI: She asked me when you were coming back.

TOPE: Reeeaaally…yeah? Jennifer, lovely Jennifer *(Snapping out of it.)* Foolish girl. I don't have time for that. My studies come first. If I don't pass the exams, I can't come home. This school is so bad, Timi. You don't know what I'm going through.

TIMI: But you got a nice room?

TOPE: Room? I'm in a dorm.

TIMI: How many in there?

TOPE: Wale, Bolaji, Bradley – he's from America – Colin from Australia, Jason. Oh yeah. Jason. I forgot to tell you. He's from your endz, you know. He used to be in the Cashing Up Crew.

TIMI: Jason... Jason... Oh yeah, he had that pit bull that bit Stephan one time.

TOPE: Yeah, that Jason.

TOPE: He's the head of our house. Gonna be head boy, he reckons. But I'm gonna get that position. So that's one, two, three, four, five and me. So six.

TIMI: You all have to sleep in the same room?

TOPE nods.

TIMI: What if someone farts?

TOPE: They do. But, bruv, I'm too tired to notice. We have to get up at 6am, go for a 30 minute run, come back, do early morning chores, get washed and have breakfast. Then we start lessons at 8, have a break at 10.30, have lessons again from 10.45 till 12.30. Then we have lunch. Lessons again, and then, after school you've got to do activities.

TIMI: What, you can't watch TV or play Playstation?

TOPE: What Playstation! I'm in Cadets on Monday, Music Club Tuesday, Chess Club Wednesday, Debating Society Thursday and Rifle Club on Friday. Then, after activities, we have to do three hours prep every night.

TIMI: At least you get weekends off.

TOPE: We have school on SATURDAY too, bruv. And we have to wash our own clothes.

TIMI: No way!

TOPE: By hand! Look at my hands. Feel them! Timi, I ain't even finished telling you what I'm going through. If I don't pass the exams at the end of the year, I have to repeat the same year until I pass. It's wicked.

TIMI: Nah. You can leave school when you're 16. That's the law, cuz.

TOPE: Not here. In my class there's mans there aged 18, 19, even a 20-year-old.

TIMI: What? With 15 year olds?

TOPE: If you don't pass the exams, they keep you in the same class till you do. Don't matter how old you are. I don't know how my mum could do this to me.

TIMI: Nah, I'd sue.

TOPE: But that's what they do here. I'm telling you.

TIMI: Nah, nah. You got rights. Human rights.

TOPE: I know. But this is Nigeria. And that Principal…he don't play.

TIMI: Yeah, I felt the brother.

TOPE: 'Act as though you're in the early days of a better nation.'

TIMI: Whassat?

TOPE: I don't know! 'Act as though you're in the early days of a better nation.' That's what he makes us say every day in assembly. He's bonkers. The whole place is unreal. You gotta wear your uniform exactly right. Gotta do all the work on time. Gotta get the most As…one boy, that Wale in my dorm – man is waking me up at 5am in the morning. 'Tope, let's read together!' But…

He pauses, bites his lip, looks over shyly at TIMI.

TIMI: What?

TOPE: Nothing.

TIMI: Tell me!

TOPE: Well, this term … I came top in all my classes.

TIMI: Shut up, boffin, or I'll put you in your coffin.

TOPE: *(Laughing.)* That's sick. You still rhyming?

TIMI: I wrote that in Maths. I do about two every lesson.

TOPE: You were the best writer in our class. Mr Carter loved off your essays.

TIMI: Shuuuut up. I aint no nerd. Oi, who's the best MC in your class?

TOPE: *(Shrugging.)* Nobody. They're not into that.

TIMI: Who's the best fighter?

TOPE: Fighter? They hit you with a cane if you even talk in class.

TIMI: Say what?

TOPE: They hit you! They flog you in front of assembly if you're really bad.

TIMI: That's child abuse!

TOPE: But nobody really talks in class. We just work.

TIMI: If any teacher hit me at school…!

TOPE: At first, I was like 'where's the social services? Where's the social worker?' And they were like, 'This is Nigeria. You're on your own!'

TIMI: I would have run away.

TOPE: I was trying to. Every day! I was hungry all the time. I didn't like the food. And, oh my days, the heat! It was killing me. Then I just thought, I'm the one making myself ill. I can't run far like that, can I? Might as well play along, pretend to like it.

TIMI: I would never let them break me. Fight the power!

TOPE: Then…about Easter time, I think…yeah, just before the end of the second term – I got a good mark for some geography and I got praised in front of the whole school. I was, like, top. Top of the class. Me? Tope, top! I never thought I could do that. It was a funny feeling. They were all cheering, and the Principal! He was crying. He was, for real. And the girls here, they admire you. Like, it's cool to be clever. I dunno. I just started getting on with it. Timi-man, let me wear your hat?

TIMI: Move, man. Get your own stuff. What do I look like? Footlocker?

TOPE: Now *(Hesitant.)* sometimes… I enjoy class.

TIMI: Yeah, yeah. Course. Sometimes I do wanna work too. But then I hear Lil Wayne or Tupac and their songs come rushing into my head and all I can think about is money and cars and girls, the bling, the garms and I just wanna be rich and live just like them. Go to Hollywood…

TOPE: I'm going America too. To Yale.

They sit in silence for a beat.

TOPE: Come to think of it, nobody ever talks in class. What gets you respect at home is a disgrace here.

TIMI nods.

TIMI: Nutters back home, man. When you think about it, really and truly, I gotta admit, being here has made me sort of think…how we carry on sometimes, like going mad on the bus home from school…fighting and madness…and the adults just sit there or get off, too scared to say anything, or the conductor stops the bus till we get off…all the fighting… over stupid stuff. It's like every day someone's hurt…your mum send you out here just after they killed Rio, innit? But since then, more and more and more… I've lost count.

TOPE: I saw all that stuff on the internet. How many boys?

TIMI: I dunno, you know. Mostly stabbings. Altogether…it's a lot.

TOPE: What's up with that?

TIMI: Same old, same old. Just beef, innit. I got mugged in the park few months back.

TOPE: Yeah?

TIMI: Third time. I told my mum I lost my phone. But that's how come I got this new one, so it worked out OK.

TOPE: Didn't you have back-up?

TIMI: Yeah. I was on my way back from football with Stephan and Luke. But there was about ten of them. Took Luke's chain, one he got for Christmas from his dad, Stephan's birthday money, my new football boots…my predators…

TOPE: Crazy.

TIMI: And all the newspapers and stuff are going, 'ooh, teenage killings. Ooh, Teenagers killing teenagers. How terrible. How shocking. How awful.' Telling us we should hand in our knives! Like that's gonna make any difference.

TOPE: It might.

TIMI: Never. It won't happen. But they just don't get it. Like my mum. She thinks life is all peace and love. Like hippie days. Maybe in the olden times they could go out and play in the park and not get beef. But nowadays? Forget dat! Everyone wants stuff. The latest this, the latest that. And they ain't got money. So they just take it. Well, that's last time I'm being held up. I'll be ready for them next time.

TOPE: How?

TIMI: Nah, it's alright. I best just keep it to myself.

TOPE: Is it what you were gonna tell me before? Tell me.

TIMI: If you blab or grass me up…

TOPE: On my life. Tell me, man.

TIMI: Swear on your mum's life.

TOPE: I swear on my mum's life.

TIMI: OK. Well, yeah, we got a replica gun.

TOPE: What? Where from?

TIMI: Off the internet. And in Design and Technology class, I learned how to convert it so it'll work for real.

TOPE: Timi, I don't think you should do that.

TIMI: What?

TOPE: I'm serious. That's stupid. You're gonna get yourself killed.

TIMI: Stupid? Damn. In school, you were the man. YOU used to be a badman.

TOPE: Yeah, back then…but look at me now.

TIMI: What the hell happened to you?

TOPE: What the hell happened to you! That's all bullshit. We're not mobsters, we ain't gangsters. We're schoolboys. Think of the future.

TIMI: OK, OK. Whatever. Calm down. I'll only use it in self-defence. And I'm joining a fam. Strength in numbers. You gotta roll deep, these days.

TOPE: You…joining a gang?

TIMI: The Hoodlums. My initiation's next week.

TOPE: Timi, have you gone mad? YOU? In a fam???

TIMI: YOU used to be in one. Anyway, I know what I'm doing. Just till I finish school and move out of the area. I can't survive on my own, can I?

TOPE: Don't be stupid. That's not how to survive.

TIMI: Stop calling me stupid! What do you know, anyway? In your stupid Harry Potter boarding school, doing debating and chess and that crap.

TOPE: I don't want you to die.

TIMI: Well, I'm not gonna, am I? Anyway, give me my trainers back.

TOPE: Your mum would go mental.

TIMI: I'm 16 next week. I can do what I want.

End of scene four.

SCENE FIVE

It's 9.25. MAMA-RONKE and BEV are in the front room with TOYIN, SIS RONKE and PRIN OSUN. MAMA is sorting the tickets and passports.

TOYIN is pacing up and down.

PRIN OSUN: To be frank, I'm very surprised. I didn't expect this. Well, if you're not sure…perhaps…

TOYIN: Let me just think about it, please. I don't know…

BEV: Sign.

MAMA-RONKE: Sign.

SIS RONKE: Sign and let us move on, for goodness' sake. The driver is ready to pack everything in the car. What is all this nonsense!

TOYIN: But after what you and mum are going through…?

SIS RONKE: That's different. Timi is not 3.

PRIN OSUN: OK. You know what, I have to collect one other boy from near Leventis suya. Let me come back in ten minutes. When I do, I want a decision.

As he leaves, BABA enters hurriedly.

BABA: I've got it! At last. I've got it!

PRIN OSUN: *(Prostrating.)* E kaale. Good evening, sah.

BABA acknowledges him with a nod. PRIN OSUN exits.

TOYIN runs over to BABA.

TOYIN: Oh, Uncle.

BABA: You didn't sign?

TOYIN: *(Tearful.)* No. Not yet.

BABA: Thank goodness!

TOYIN: But I don't know. What they're saying. Maybe, maybe, there's some truth in it.

MAMA-RONKE: Brother, I beg: don't advise her any more.

TOYIN: Maybe it's for the best, Uncle. I've got to think ahead, what's best for Timi's future; the kind of man I want him to be?

BABA: No, no. I've seen it. Finally! I can see what you are trying to do and why it is wrong.

TOYIN: What?

BABA: You are trying to turn the clock back.

TOYIN: The clock?

BABA: Yes, yes. And you cannot do that. You cannot.

MAMA-RONKE: More wahala!

BABA: Pandora, please. I knew there was something deeper, and now I've seen it.

He scoops up his agbada and sits down.

BABA: Toyin, listen to me. Listen to me well, well. The fears you were expressing are real. You know you do not belong here, neither does your son.

MAMA-RONKE: He belongs here! They both do.

BABA: Sister, you yourself, someone who was born and raised here, after so many years in London, do you really still belong?

MAMA-RONKE: I do. What are you talking? I'm still a Nigerian.

BABA: Do you really feel at home in Nigeria?

MAMA-RONKE: Ah ah. Yes, of course I do.

BABA: Iro! You do not. I saw you. I watched you, looking around, eyes up and down when we visited Chief Ogunyinka in Apapa last week. I could read you when you were a child. I can still read you now. You were appalled, were you not? The area has gone so far down, so low, you almost didn't recognize his house.

MAMA-RONKE: Well, of course, it was a shock. I admit. I said so openly. Compared to how I remember it. When we used to pick mangoes from his father's garden as children, it was like Eden to me.

BABA: And when we visited the old government hospital on Ikorodu Road, where you did your nursing training with Professor Brown? I saw the disappointment in your eyes. Tell the truth.

MAMA-RONKE: Yes, yes, things have changed...

BABA: I am your elder brother. You are my aburo. And what I see I must say. Timi does not belong here.

MAMA-RONKE: Broda, he is an African.

BABA: No, he is not. *(Taking a passport from MAMA.)* This is his passport. Red p, abi? He is British! He is not a Yoruba. He is… Euroba.

TOYIN: Huh?

BABA: You were born in Europe. Your son was born in Europe. Stay there.

MAMA-RONKE: What if they were born on the moon? Would that make them Martians? Bev, help me, o. I'm too tired…

BEV: You don't have to live where you were born.

BABA: You're an adult, making a choice to move. And, by the way, you're always complaining that Oyinbo discriminate against you. That they don't see you as English. Why should they? Look how you're deserting them. Just because things are getting tough down there.

BEV: The plane was full of white people coming to Africa. Wasn't it, Auntie Pandora? They're leaving too!

MAMA-RONKE: It was. I was so surprised.

BABA: Did Nigeria educate you? No, England did! So use your skills there. If you want to be equal, commit, stick it out, as Oyinbo do. Work to make changes there.

BEV: Uncle, I'd love to contribute to my country. I've tried to. But do they want my contribution? Well, I refuse to be wasted!

BABA: But you are one of them. You are English.

BEV: I am. I know. I know. Every room I walk into, England walks in too. Every word I speak, England speaks too. That's what it is. I am what I am. But I can't grow there. Honestly, Uncle, I can't achieve what I'm capable of. And I know what I'm capable of. And it's not just about my career. I'm… we're … more than English. I want to discover another part of me. My other side. And how life is here.

BABA: The world is a market place. There is no promised land. But, you will see. *(To TOYIN.)* Timi doesn't want to come here, does he?

TOYIN shakes her head.

BABA: Then listen to him. Let him decide. He is a human being.

SIS-RONKE: How can he decide? The parent has to choose for the child. She is his mother. She has to choose *(She pauses, computing something.)* …she has to choose what she thinks is best… Oh…she has to choose… *(She looks at MAMA.)* …what she thinks…oh…is best for the child.

She looks from MAMA to TOYIN.

BEV: Exactly! She has to weigh up the options and decide. No one's got a crystal ball.

SIS RONKE: No crystal ball. *(To BEV.)* That's right. She can only do what she thinks is right. It's obvious.

RONKE gets up and paces, watching the others.

BABA: *(To TOYIN.)* I know this school you are considering is for ajebota, for the elite. They have nice buildings and so on and so forth. But those schools are modeled on British schools in the first place. Most of them were founded during the colonial period by missionaries. Most of them are still run by Oyinbo. The headmasters are mostly English. They insist the children speak only English. They are like mini-Englands! Why bring him from England for more England? Does it make sense?

TOYIN: Yes! That's what I've been saying.

BABA: Good. So you know. Those kids they bring from overseas, they cope, yes, on the whole. Because they have to. They make good contacts, yes, most of them, they go to the best universities in Africa, in Europe, in America. And then what? Are their lives any better for it? Pulled up from their roots at a most crucial point in their lives. How do they actually feel inside for the rest of their days? Spending the last stage of childhood in a foreign land? Without friends and family they know?

MAMA-RONKE: He is not a foreigner. And the friends he has in London are not real friends. They are the ones leading him down the wrong path.

BABA: *(To TOYIN.)* Where a tree grows, it stays. Yes, you can move a baby plant and it can grow. But the man who's been transplanted, he cannot. Timi is no longer a baby. I'm warning you, for the sake of your son, take him back.

TOYIN: England isn't paradise.

BABA: But why run away? It's your country. Stay and fight. Fight for his rights.

TOYIN: I've been fighting since he was born.

BABA: Then keep fighting! No matter. Fight on. Fight better. Don't come running back to Africa when the going gets tough. Is that what you want to teach him? To run?

BEV: Uncle, it's a really hard system.

BABA: You think England is hard? Compared to Nigeria? My dear, you haven't seen anything yet!

BEV: You're in Africa. You don't understand about racism. You can't.

BABA: I understand! Come on! Such people – they are always with us. Rise above them! Excellence is the best response.

BEV: Our boys are dying on the streets every day.

BABA: So every African child in England is failing. All of them?

BEV: No, but…

BABA: Eh heh. So what is the difference between the ones that fail and the ones that don't?

BEV: The parent, the school, the child all play a part…

BABA: So find a better school, and work with him, turn him around… Toyin, you can do it. Don't give up on him. Don't ask strangers to do what you should do yourself.

TOYIN: Maybe I could get him a better tutor, and a mentor. I could do more one-to-one with him. Personal development work. Find out what he really wants…

BEV: Toyin, no…Uncle, Timi's got to a point where…he's got into a situation…and this isn't just about grades. Here, he'll be studying African history, African philosophy, literature, art – he won't get that in any school in England.

BABA: Didn't I just tell you that school is modeled on English public schools? You want African culture? Take him to Peckham!

BEV: He'll be a better man in Africa.

BABA: This is nonsense! Am I not an African man? What is so special about African men?

TOYIN: African men do not abandon their children.

MAMA-RONKE: Excuse me? What of your father?

TOYIN: Yeah, OK. But how many do that?

MAMA-RONKE: He did. Useless bastard.

BABA: Who asked you to stay in London? They sent you there to study. You were supposed to come back. Our mother begged you to come home. We built you a house, we sent you tickets. But you refused point blank. This is all your doing.

MAMA-RONKE: Everyone is blaming me, as usual.

BABA: Well, what's done is done. And maybe it's for the best. Look what Nigeria has become anyway! Maybe you people who abandoned us were right. The wheel is still turning. Yes, you're struggling – for a few generations of course you will – but something will come of it all. *(To TOYIN.)* Whatever the reason you people were born down there, the future will reveal. Each generation must first discover its mission, then fulfill it.

BEV: We're supposed to be talking about Timi?

BABA: Yes, Timi is what matters. *(Gripping TOYIN's hand.)* Rotimi's life is still in your hands; you have to choose for him. Don't spoil it for him! Don't turn back. Keep going. Whatever the problems you face, he is in an advanced society with many opportunities. You can guide him to access them. Don't make the wrong choice and ruin his life forever, o.

TOYIN: Yes! That's just what I've been saying. I told them I've changed my mind and they won't accept it. They're the one's pressuring me. I'm right. I know what I'm doing.

BEV: This is his last chance, it will be too late…

TOYIN: *(Flinging the brochure aside.)* Transformation chamber. Torture chamber, more like! Look how scared Topsy was of that man! They cane kids! They beat them.

BEV: I'm warning you.

TOYIN: Mum, gimme Timi's passport. He's coming home.

MAMA-RONKE: She's right.

TOYIN: Just because you abandoned your child, you want me to do the same. Well, I'm not a bad mother like you!

MAMA-RONKE: Toyin!

TOYIN: *(Taking it.)* Give me his passport!

BEV: That's harsh, Toyin.

TOYIN: And you? What do you know about being a mother? You're just jealous. Can you even have children?

BEV: Jealous, am I?

TOYIN: Yes.

BEV: Well, I'm glad I don't have a son who's posting messages on the internet about killing people.

TOYIN: What?

BEV: You have the cheek to insult me, but do you know who and what your child really is? Well, let me show you. I got onto his Facebook page last month. And guess what I found out about your little angel?

She takes out her phone and begins pounding at the keys.

BEV: Come and see for yourself what your CHILD is up to.

TOYIN: What you talking about?

BEV: Come and see!

TOYIN goes over and takes the phone. She gasps. MAMA-RONKE looks too.

MAMA-RONKE: Let me see. Oludumare!

TOYIN: Maybe it's not him.

MAMA-RONKE: That's him.

BEV: He's behind the one holding the gun.

Reality dawns on TOYIN. She clasps the phone, dizzy.

TOYIN: Timi?

MAMA-RONKE: Bev, what is this?

BEV: That's the site for a gang in our area. They put all their nonsense on the internet.

BABA: You mean he is a gang member?

BEV: Nearly.

TOYIN: How did you know?

BEV: A few months back, I was over at your house and when I went to get your laptop from his room, I saw him reading a magazine about guns. He was cutting out adverts. He put it away quickly, but I saw a few of them when they fell on the floor.

BABA: A gang member?

The doorbell rings.

SIS RONKE: TAOFIKI! Open the door.

TOYIN: Why didn't you tell me?

BABA: Rotimi? A gang member?

BEV: You would have confronted him, and then he would never have come to Nigeria.

TOYIN: Oh, my god!

MAMA: Joh, why are you still talking? Sign the papers!

BABA: No, this is when he needs you, his mother, more than ever. Take him back to London.

MAMA-RONKE: What, even now? You still insist.

BABA: Especially now. Work with him. Don't reject him at this his time of crisis. When he needs you most. You are his mother.

TOYIN looks from one face to another, searching for the answer. But it's not on any of their faces, it's within.

TOYIN: Baba, I don't know how to help him. I need help.

BABA: Pah. I can't say anymore.

PRIN OSUN enters.

PRIN OSUN: The traffic is getting worse. I have to set off.

TOYIN: Wait. Wait.

PRIN OSUN: You can't delay me any longer. If you don't want the place...

TOYIN: Yes, yes, I do.

PRIN OSUN: Please, the papers, are they ready?

TOYIN: Yes.

She grabs the pen and signs. PRIN OSUN picks up the paper and scans it.

PRIN OSUN: Good. I'll be right back to collect him. I'll beep three times. Send him down and we'll be off before he knows what's happening.

TOYIN nods grimly, still studying the picture.

TOYIN: Timi. Timi.

He exits. TOYIN takes the uniform and puts it back into TIMI's case.

TOYIN: *(To BEV.)* That's why you insisted on coming here with us?

BEV: I had to make sure you went through with it.

TOYIN nods. She's trembling.

TOYIN: I've failed.

BEV: No! We've all failed. Society. Now let them fix him.

TIMI and TOPE enter.

TIMI: Hi Mum.

They sit. TOYIN looks at TIMI. She doesn't answer. He looks around.

TIMI: What's the matter with everyone… Oh, you're talking about my birthday surprise.

TOYIN: Where's your suitcase, Bev?

BEV: I'm staying.

TOYIN: I'm sorry about what I said. I didn't mean it…

BEV: I just want to change my life too.

TOYIN: Mum, listen to Bev.

MAMA-RONKE: She already decided. If she insists on staying, then there's nothing we can do. She's an adult.

TIMI: I'll be an adult too, next week.

SIS RONKE: *(To BEV.)* I have to meet him, this your so-called Dayo.

BEV: He's just pulling up. Go over to the window.

SIS-RONKE: *(To MAMA.)* O ye ko so fun Timi nisiyi. K'o mo pe o nlo pelu Principal ati Tope k'o bale ni igba die ti o ma fi mo l'ara. [*I think she should tell Timi now. He should know that he's leaving with the Principal and Tope, so he can have a few moments to get used to the idea.*]

MAMA-RONKE: *(Nodding.)* Since he's going soon, she must tell him.

TOPE's eyes widen.

TOYIN: *(To SIS RONKE.)* What did you say?

SIS RONKE: *(In English.)* Why don't you learn your language? A Yoruba girl who can't speak Yoruba! It's a pity.

She points to the boys.

SIS RONKE: I'll translate later.

BEV: *(Checking phone.)* He's here. Go to the window.

She exits. TOPE looks at TIMI and nudges him. TIMI looks at him bewildered.

TIMI: What?

TOPE: You're in trouble, bruv.

He drags TIMI off to the side, out of their earshot.

TOPE: Well, well, well. Life is full of surprises.

TIMI: What you on about?

TOPE: I wonder why your suitcase is the only one left?

TIMI: Is it? Oh yeah. They must have forgotten. So?

TOPE: Did they forget or didn't they? I wonder.

TIMI: Well, of course they forgot. It's got my stuff in it for next week.

TOPE: Like what?

TIMI: Got my boots for football on Tuesday. Some stuff for my party. What you smiling for?

TOPE: Yep, OK, football on Tuesday? You sure about that?

TIMI: What is wrong with you?

TOPE: First, let me have your trainers.

TIMI: You're mad. Move, man.

TOPE: OK, OK. Just give me the hat.

TIMI: Yeah, you can have it. It's a fake anyway.

He takes it off and TOPE plonks it on his own head.

TIMI: Yeah, so what's the news?

TOPE: You won't be anywhere near football club next week. Or London. Or England

TIMI: What you on about?

TOPE: Because you're coming to my school.

TIMI: Don't be stupid. Gimme my hat.

TOPE: That's what they were just talking about. Your mum is leaving you behind.

He snatches the hat back.

TIMI: You're lying.

TOPE: Am I though?

TIMI looks over at the case – the penny drops.

TIMI: Oh no. That uniform!

TOPE: This is just what they did to me too. A holiday, they said. Then bam!

TIMI: You grassed me up, didn't you?

TOPE: When could I have grassed? I didn't say anything.

TIMI: *(Furious.)* You better not have.

TOPE: I didn't. I swear.

TIMI: How could she? My own mum.

TOPE: I've got your back. But first…

TIMI holds out the phone. TOPE takes it.

TOPE: Sweet. This is how you're gonna roll…

They exit, whispering, as BEV enters, smirking.

BEV: Have you seen him?

MAMA-RONKE: Who?

BEV: He can't find parking, but he's downstairs.

SIS RONKE, MAMA and TOYIN go to the window and lean out.

SIS RONKE: That man by the petrol station?

BEV: No, in front of the fruit stall.

SIS RONKE: You mean… *(She inhales.)* HIM!

TOYIN: That one in the linen suit, Bev? HIM!

BEV: Yep.

MAMA-RONKE: *(Fanning herself.)* Oh, my goodness.

BEV watches their reactions. She was right. He is the most gorgeous male on earth.

SIS RONKE: *(Shouting out.)* So, good evening, Mr Dipo…

BEV: *(Hissing.)* Dapo.

SIS RONKE: Dipo, Dapo. Joh! Mr man, you know who I am, abi? I asked to meet you because, as you know, this *(She points to BEV.)* is my sister's friend. Maybe she's from Jamaica…

BEV: Antigua!

SIS RONKE: Ah ah. Wetin! Antigua. Jamaica. Let me do what I should do. *(To DAPO.)* As I was saying, maybe you think she has nobody here to represent her. But she is a daughter of this house. Shog bo me? Any funny business, any 419er antics, and this our Lagos won't be big enough for the both of us. Sho get?

SIS RONKE folds her arms and leans back, studying him.

SIS RONKE: Go and park; we'll speak seriously later.

Just then TIMI bursts back into the room, followed by TOPE.

TIMI: Mum! Look.

They all turn from the window. He prostrates wildly, doing all variations, from the slight bow to the final all-the-way-down one when he's practically rolling on the floor.

TOYIN: What are you doing?

TIMI: I can prostrate. Look, mum. Tope taught me. Look, Aunty Ronke.

He rolls/prostrates again.

SIS RONKE: Better late than never. Well done.

TIMI: Did I do it right, mum?

TOYIN: *(Sadly.)* Very nice, Timi.

There are three loud beeps from downstairs.

TIMI: Mum, mum, mum. Don't leave me behind.

TOYIN: I have to, my darling. Timi, I've been lying to myself. But not any more. You're going to stay. This is a chance for you to change your ways.

TIMI: No, mum, no.

TOYIN: You'll retake your GCSEs, then come home for A levels and university.

TIMI: No, no. Don't do this. It's not fair. Why do I have to lose all my friends?

TOYIN: I saw your Facebook page.

TIMI's face drops.

TOYIN: Guns, Timi. Guns.

TIMI: They weren't real, mum.

TOYIN: They were.

TIMI: I mean… I mean…they weren't loaded.

TOYIN: Haven't I taught you that life is something precious?

TIMI: Mum, mum, we were just posing… It's not even mine… Stefan found it…it's just a replica…

He's babbling, frantic, but from her frozen gaze he knows he's busted. Game over.

TOYIN: I want you to amount to something, Timi. To grow into a man. A good man. A decent man.

The beeps start again.

85

TIMI: Mum, I know life is precious, and I was just trying to protect mine. You don't know what it's like. I know what I'm doing. Just trust me.

TOYIN: Trust you?

TIMI: You're right. It was a mistake. I've made a mistake. I'm sorry. OK? But I can change, I can change without staying here. I swear. I can sort it out.

TOYIN: You're staying.

TIMI: Just believe in me, Mum. I've learned my lesson. I can change in London. I can do anything.

TOYIN: You'll prove that by doing well in school here.

TIMI's face crumples.

TIMI: Mum, please. My dad left me, now you.

It's her Achilles heel, and he knows it. He's playing his last card. She gulps and looks down, shaking a little.

TIMI: If you really love me, don't leave me too, Mum. You said you believed in me.

TOYIN: *(She looks up, nodding.)* I do.

TIMI: So believe I can change. Help me.

TOYIN: That's what I intend to do. I need help to help you.

TIMI: What do you know about my life? About what I have to do to survive? You can't do this to me. You can't do this to me.

TOYIN stands there like steel, immovable. TIMI runs to BEV. She hugs and kisses him.

BEV: *(Sadly.)* Sorry, babes.

He runs to MAMA.

TIMI: Granny, please!

MAMA-RONKE: *(She clasps him.)* My wonderful, be a good boy.

TIMI: Uncle!

BABA: Do as your mother says.

We hear footsteps and PRIN OSUN enters, agitated.

PRIN OSUN: Can't you hear the car? We're ready. Let's go.

He gestures to TOPE to pick up TIMI's case while he prises TIMI from MAMA's arms.

PRIN OSUN: Let go of him. Let him GO!

He clasps TIMI's hand in an iron grip. TIMI tries to wriggle out but resistance is futile. TOYIN holds out her arms to hug TIMI. He pushes her off.

TOYIN: I'll come back to see you at Christmas.

TIMI: I hate you.

TOYIN: I love you. And I still believe in you.

TIMI: I'll never forgive you. Never. I hate you. I hate all of you. It's my life!

PRIN OSUN: Oya!

TIMI is led off, sobbing. TOYIN moves to follow them. SIS RONKE stops her.

SIS RONKE: Let me.

She exits after them. BEV follows. TOYIN sinks into the sofa. The umbilical cord is finally cut and she's lost. BEV looks on, stunned it finally happened. BABA picks up TIMI's hat from the floor. He plonks it on his head.

BABA: Ah well. That is that. I'll go there tomorrow to visit him. And I may as well come to the airport and see you people off. Let me get my car.

He exits.

BEV: I'll tell Dapo we're leaving.

BEV follows him.

TOYIN starts to sob. MAMA-RONKE comes over and cradles her. They sit like this for some moments.

MAMA-RONKE: I know how you're feeling.

TOYIN: My baby.

SIS RONKE returns, but they don't see her.

MAMA-RONKE: I know. I went through the same thing. But it is for the best. You want the best for him. You're doing it because you love your child.

SIS RONKE looks at them, and shrinks back. TOYIN looks up and sees her.

She stretches out her hand to her. SIS RONKE comes in and takes her hand. She holds it, awkwardly.

SIS RONKE: You did the right thing.

MAMA-RONKE: Did she?

SIS RONKE: People can only do what they think is right. Anyway, sha, my life is OK. Why should I complain?

MAMA-RONKE: My dear.

They embrace. But it's getting a bit mushy for RONKE.

SIS RONKE: You people will miss your flight to London. TAOFIKI! Where is my handbag?

MAMA picks up the handbag from the sofa and hands it to her.

MAMA-RONKE: Let him relax.

SIS RONKE: *(Taking it.)* OK, OK. *(Calling out.)* Taofiki, go and rest. Do you hear? Rest! Ma'mi, oya *[let's go].*

She holds out her hand for MAMA who takes it, smiling. They leave. TOYIN sits still. BEV enters and sits on the sofa. The women look at each other. Then they hug.

TOYIN: Thank you.

BEV: Don't thank me. Thank your family. The family who you don't know, who don't know you, who see you as a tourist, who you don't belong with…

TOYIN: I must have been nuts!

TOYIN gives BEV TIMI's passport.

TOYIN: Look after our son.

BEV: Ah ah, of course, now!

TOYIN: I want to let mum and Sis Ronke drive together.

BEV: OK. Daps will take us. Come on.

TOYIN: I hope it works out with you two.

BEV: It will. And for Timi. And for you.

She hugs TOYIN.

BEV: We did it!

She flies out the door.

The room is empty again. TOYIN stands alone, in exactly the spot she started in when we first met her. But the confusion and stress is gone. She takes a deep breath, looks upwards and mouths:

TOYIN: Thank you.

There are beeps from outside. She takes one last look around, closes the trunk, and leaves.

The End.